The Connecting Leader

The Connecting Leader

In the Age of Hyper-Transparency,
Interconnectivity and Media Anarchy,
How Corporate Leaders Connect
Business with Society

Alberto Lopez Valenzuela

THE CONNECTING LEADER
In the Age of Hyper-Transparency, Interconnectivity and Media Anarchy, How Corporate Leaders Connect Business with Society

ISBN 978-1-5445-1250-1 *Paperback*
978-1-5445-1249-5 *Ebook*

To Madalina, the strongest person I know and
to Alma, the reason for everything.

Contents

Foreword

BY CHRIS CLARK
EX GLOBAL CMO OF HSBC & INDEPENDENT NON-EXEC

IT SEEMS TODAY THAT THE ONLY THING THAT STAYS THE same and is certain is the ever-constant beat of the drum of change. We can wake up every morning and see for ourselves a different landscape and set of opportunities and options. Business models are in flux, traditional areas are being constantly disrupted and historically strong businesses are fighting for their survival. So, whether we run major corporations, are successful entrepreneurs, provide wisdom and guidance to others or simply consider what the business world will be like for the next generation, the march of change is irresistible. It is also moving at a pace that means we all need to adapt, and we all need to find a new level of resilience to thrive and prosper.

This 'New Normal' as explored in The Connecting Leader outlines a healthier and fairer place to do business. The corporate kimono is wide open and never before have we seen such a transparent environment in which to do business. The power and reach of social media and the tools of the modern digital business world mean there are no places to hide. Those who might choose to try and spin bad news, cover up unsavoury practices or cut corners by short-changing customers will find themselves outed and exposed. This is surely a good thing and ensures a playing field that produces worthy winners. The basic success formula is clear; brands need to provide good, clear value in their contract with customers, products and propositions must meet customers' needs and businesses need to be clear that their contribution runs beyond just profit. This construct is ably illustrated in The Connecting Leader with some sound examples of modern businesses that have adapted to this agenda well and continue to thrive.

The clear message is that the fundamental strength of a sound set of values and purpose are what underpins the healthy and prospering organisation of today. It guides their people's day-to-day actions, helps them recruit and retain talent, provides a platform of trust in the contract with customers and ensures stakeholders such as regulators, commentators and shareholders understand them fully and value them and their contribution.

But…and it is a big but, the complexity of the 'New Normal' transparent landscape, the speed and motion of change and the competitive nature of the market places we operate in need a new kind of leadership with a new set of capabilities. This force is at the heart of the Connecting Leader principle. Organisations of any scale and ambition will need to understand how to identify and value individuals capable of being their Connecting Leaders. They will need to nurture the concept as a management competence. It is important that they use as many external markers to manage as they do internal. Understanding the construct of a positive reputation as a by-product of this job well done, as well as having a constant ear-to-the-ground way of listening to those important to you, is not optional. All this needs to be achieved with a genuine, unconscious authenticity at the heart of the organisation. You can't manufacture this gold dust of authenticity, you need to allow it to emerge, and it is the very life blood of The Connecting Leader. How you might do this and what you need to consider are covered exceptionally well in this excellent book.

So let me tell you a tale that has stayed with me for a few years now and still strikes a chord. I was at a conference and during a break I fell into conversation with someone who clearly had a touch of the giant ego about them. They asked what I was doing about my own personal development and I am sure I babbled on about staying ahead of the digital curve and absorbing myself in how this was spawning the then embryonic Fin Tech category. He raised an eye brow. "Well that's all well and good," said he as he proudly puffed up his chest and finished with, "I'm working very hard on being authentic..." Hmmmmm! Perhaps his lack of Connecting Leader DNA will unseat him, but if I can find him again, I think I should put a copy of this book in his hand and suggest that being a Connected Leader might serve him better.

So perhaps consider the following as you reflect on your working world. Do you wake up in the morning and are able to say to yourself 'Today is different and what was there yesterday is no more...hurrah! That is so cool'? Can you say 'I have at my fingertips all the information I need in real time to get a pretty good picture of what is going on, and I have the ability to mobilise and connect with some great people to get things done' or even 'I am working on being a proper Connecting Leader who has a clear understanding of the authenticity of the business I am in and fully understand its values and purpose'? If you can say 'yes' or would like to say 'yes', then give this book a go. It will lift a few scales from your eyes and provide a grounded and well-proven set of principles that will endure.

Alberto writes with an engaging style and makes his points with living examples. His passion for the principles in this book are clear and he has a track record that proves his points. He also happens to be a naturally authentic and connected leader himself, and he is also someone I am proud to call friend.

INTRODUCTION

CHANGE CREATES OPPORTUNITY

IN FEBRUARY 2009, IN THE AFTERMATH OF THE FINANCIAL crisis, I was fired. Luckily, I was able to take time to think about what I should and shouldn't do next. After a few weeks of deliberation, I reached the conclusion that I had no desire to rush back to corporate life. Instead, I decided to start a business, which led to the beginning of the most fulfilling, intense and happiest years of my professional career so far.

If we rewind back to 2009, we see the world had suffered the biggest financial crisis in its history. According to Pew Research, in the United States alone, the financial crisis cost an estimated $648 billion due to slower economic growth and federal government spending to mitigate the crisis through the Troubled Asset Relief Program (TARP), and resulted in a net cost to taxpayers of $73 billion. Plus, 5.5 million American jobs were lost. Undoubtedly, this caused the erosion of trust between Big Business and Society and set the tone for the years to come. Issues such as excessive executive pay, tax evasion schemes and anti-globalisation became regular stories in media outlets around the world.

Despite the fact that business has been one of the most powerful drivers of progress over centuries and has played a central role in improving the quality of life of millions of people, the social contract between business and society was breached and the balance of power changed from institutions to civil society. Scrutiny of Big Business by individuals intensified and businesses have never been held so accountable.

This unstoppable change has been fuelled by the *New Normal* (see Chapter Two), an interconnected, hyper-transparent and media-anarchic context that emerged from the Digital Revolution of the last twenty-five years. There was no roadmap to help companies navigate in the new context; top executives running business powerhouses did not fully grasp that in order to win in the New Normal, operating separately from society was no longer an option, leaving companies confused and struggling to understand and adapt. The "business of business" was no longer just "business." To preserve and enhance corporate value, it was essential to maintain a healthy and balanced contract with society.

As all of this was going on, my partners and I believed that a new kind of intelligence was needed for businesses to help them navigate this new environment. This intelligence would help senior leaders understand to what extent stakeholder perception was increasing or eroding corporate value. We coined this category *Reputation Intelligence*.

DISCOVERY

In the past ten years, in my role as a CEO of alva, I've become fascinated by the concept and the effect that reputation has on businesses and stakeholders. Over these years, I have pored over the research, worked with many leading corporate reputation professionals and—alongside a highly talented team—have built a successful business. With the founding of alva, we set out to help organisations better understand their stakeholders and the issues that create or erode value in their business. During this continuous process of discovery, we have identified many key insights that have shaped my thinking.

In the aftermath of the financial crisis and in response to the intense scrutiny coming from society, business initiated a process to repair the damage caused by the excesses of the previous years. Not all companies took the same approach to restoring trust; a few adopted a long-term perspective, some went into hiding and many continued being dominated by short-term financial goals.

The last two categories, companies that were mainly driven by short-term goals and those that tried to be invisible, didn't fully grasp what it took to succeed in the New Normal. The invisible type, motivated to avert public scrutiny by avoiding the limelight, failed to obtain stakeholder support when they needed it. The short-term type focused on restoring trust and building their reputation in the old-fashioned way, treating reputation as a construct. While previously, it was perfectly normal for companies to use spin and manipulative "reputation management" strategies to attract and engage stakeholders, in the New Normal, these techniques have become of very little use to navigate and recover from a crisis or restore the company's trust. The opposite is true: the more a company or individual uses these techniques, the more stakeholders disengage and disconnect from the company. Society is simply less credulous.

Contrast the above with the companies that have taken the long-term view, such as Apple, Unilever and Patagonia (see Chapter Four). These are what we call Authentic businesses, companies that have been operating under the same values and purpose from the outset. Most of the time, these are trustworthy organisations whose identity is well-defined and embodied by its employees, and that live by a strong set of clear and positive values to achieve a positive relationship with society. These companies make the

Social Contract the starting point of their existence, they embed distinctive ethical values and practices in the identity of the organisation, and these guide the engagement strategies with all stakeholders.

These are the companies that understand that a good reputation is an outcome that is formed by being genuine, doing what you say you are going to do and owning up to the mistakes when these happen. Fundamentally, this is the authentic engagement that society demands from business today. Companies that have adopted the above approach are readier to face the challenges of the New Normal.

An important revelation that emerged when studying the authentic business is that *the key factor that determines the Social Contract is the relationship that the company has with Profit.* This relationship (with profit) impacts the identity of the organisation and the nature of the Social Contract. Using this lens, we identified three types of companies: Profit First, Profit & Society and Society First.

Profit First companies are purpose-led organisations driven by shareholder value creation while also making a significant contribution to society. Consider Apple—it has a very distinctive identity, built on innovation, design and technology that drives progress for consumers and society.

Exemplifying the *Profit & Society* category, we find Unilever. The company stands as a model of sustainability, combined with profit and shareholder maximisation, and has become a global reference for other companies that strive to integrate sustainable processes at every step of the value chain.

In the third category, the *Society First* companies put society's interests before profits and report across a range of social and sustainability parameters. Patagonia is devoted to developing highly sustainable and durable products that don't damage the planet.

While each of these businesses operates with a different relationship to profit, they are all highly successful in their own right. Aside from their strong performance, what do these and other authentic companies have in common? These organisations have connected their values and objectives to their purpose in society and have been actively taking a stand on issues that matter to their constituents. They have combined *Authenticity* with the desire to *Connect* to a wide and complex web of stakeholders and issues.

As a result, these companies have experienced less disruption, less intrusion and fewer obstacles from stakeholders, including regulators and investors. These are the businesses that have mastered the art of connecting all of the pieces to create corporate value and achieve a harmonious balance across all stakeholders. These are businesses that have understood how to be relevant in the twenty-first century.

ENTER THE CONNECTING LEADER

One fundamental difference between authentic companies and the other two types, the invisible and the short-term, is that authentic companies understand the need to have a *Connecting* (executive) *Leader* who brings the outside-in view, develops policies to connect the business with the various stakeholders and maintains a healthy balance between the company objectives, outcomes and Social Contract.

The Connecting Leader has a deep appreciation of the issues affecting stakeholders and enables the alignment between the company and its stakeholders while ensuring that trust is preserved by all parties involved. The Connecting Leader acts as the "Society Proxy" in the executive team and is the one who has the licence and courage to ask tough questions such as: *Is this initiative really aligned with the type of business we are? What's the implication to society of taking this action? Are we doing this just to make money or because it is the right thing to do for all our stakeholders?*

Unfortunately, during our research, we found that there are just a few Connecting Leaders in Big Business today. While executives understand that the business plays an important role in society, the pressure to deliver financial returns in the short term is far more intense than the desire to invest in the building of long-term relationships with a wide range of constituents.

However, the Connecting Leader is a necessity in today's business. They are the partner that every CEO needs to facilitate a fruitful and fulfilling relationship with all the key internal and external stakeholders of the business. This role is the game changer in enabling companies to succeed in the New Normal.

As well as the connecting responsibilities that we cover in the book, the Connecting Leader must have the right environment to succeed—that is, the leadership support and a company culture that fosters responsibility, accountability and meaningful engagement.

AT A GLANCE

The book is divided into two key parts. Part One, The New Normal, comprises the first four chapters. In Chapter One, we review the Social Contract attempts that businesses have made over the last fifty years and why they have or haven't worked. We also take a look at the biggest forces in society over the last fifty years—Globalisation, Sustainability and the Digital Revolution. We cover the above three forces at length, as many of the issues that companies grapple with today have their origin in the three forces. Understanding this helps us contextualise and explain the current mood of polarisation and disconnect from society. In Chapter Two, we dive into the three dimensions of the New Normal: Hyper-Transparency, Interconnectivity and Media Anarchy. In Chapter Three, we explore the concept of the authentic business and how companies form strategic and value-creating reputations in the New Normal. The last chapter of Part One, Chapter Four, introduces three company types (Profit First, Profit & Society and Society First) based on the relationship that these companies have with profit, providing company examples for each of the three categories.

Having set the context in Part One, Part Two concentrates on the role of the Connecting Leader and the right environment to succeed. Chapter Five provides a detailed account of the Connecting Leader and the five key responsibilities that make up the role. From Chapter Six to Eight, we cover the three fundamental components that enable the success of the Connecting Leader; these are Authentic Leadership, Empowering Culture and Connected Intelligence. In Chapter Nine, we review the state-of-play of the Corporate Affairs and Communications function today, highlighting the opportunities and challenges of the current role. Finally, Chapter Ten questions the readiness of today's businesses to address the challenges of the Fourth Industrial Revolution and the role that Connecting Leaders should play in helping CEOs and executive teams to perform better in the future.

With the two-part structure, I intended to first provide substantial context to help aspiring Connecting Leaders frame the discussion with their peers. Second, I want to describe the role and the right environment with enough detail to help senior professionals understand the attributes and circumstances that will make this role a success for the individual, the business and society.

WHY ANOTHER "BUSINESS" BOOK?

One of the most fulfilling aspects of my job has been the opportunity to meet and work with many Corporate Affairs and Communications professionals in some of the largest companies in the world. While it is undeniable that these professionals play a fundamental role in their organisations, I have found multiple times that the role is not valued or elevated to its full potential. In some cases, the Corporate Affairs Director would play a senior adviser role reporting to the CEO but detached from the rest of the business. In other cases, the Chief Communications Officer would be relegated to tactical PR or crisis management. Being seen as a cost centre instead of a value-creating function will always be part of the challenge.

As the New Normal has created a new operating context in which a prerequisite of success for every company is to enjoy a good Social Contract with its key stakeholders, every company that aims to thrive over the long term must be authentic and adopt a mechanism to Connect with its stakeholders. To achieve this state, every company must have a Connecting Leader as a core member of the executive team.

With this book, I want to put a strong case forward to CEOs and the other members of the board that to actively connect the business with society and its key constituents, the Corporate Affairs Director or the Chief Communications Officer must be elevated to a more strategic position in the company. Equally, I also want to call all aspiring Connecting Leaders everywhere to recognise and seize the opportunity to step up and make the difference to the business (and themselves).

In my opinion, the New Normal has created the perfect context to catalyse this evolution of the Corporate Affairs and Communications professionals. Communication and stakeholder engagement have become a core competency that all companies must excel at to achieve a healthy relationship between business and society. These professionals are the best placed to enable the connection between the two.

PART ONE

The New Normal

"Change is inevitable. Growth is optional."

JOHN MAXWELL

CHAPTER ONE

The Social Contract

IT IS UNDENIABLE THAT BUSINESS HAS BEEN AND IS ONE of the most powerful drivers of progress over centuries in society. It has played a central role in improving the quality of life of millions of people by constantly evolving through a balancing act between government and civil society. When this relationship is harmonious, businesses are able to meet the needs of their communities and enable the prosperity of their members.

However, over the last quarter of a century, the Social Contract between business and society seems to have lost its harmony. While technological innovation and economic growth have accelerated and benefited many, there are many indicators showing that we are experiencing inequality, environmental degradation and a general loss of trust in business.[1]

One of the most testing and damaging times for the relationship between business, government and society was during the financial crisis of 2008, when the trust among the three parties was shattered.

New concerns were added to post-crisis anxiety, such as anger

1 Jay Coen Gilbert. "What Is the Role of Business in Society?". *Huffington Post*. November 11, 2015. https://www.huffingtonpost.com/jay-coen-gilbert/what-is-the-role-of-busin_b_8527530.html

about excessive executive pay, the effects of automation, tax avoidance and evasion, the unmooring of multinational companies from local communities, the power of big technology and the imbalances between gig economy paymasters and workers.[2]

We live in an environment of intense scrutiny, so concerns like these rise to the surface very quickly. Companies need to rethink the type of relationship they want to form with their stakeholders and society at large. To thrive today, companies need to reconnect with their Social Contract.

THE SOCIAL CONTRACT

Over the past fifty years, the social contract between business and society has fallen mainly into two different categories: the "maximise shareholder value" model, which still prevails and the "corporate social responsibility" model, which sought to address sustainability issues. A similar distinction was made by Sue Garrard from Unilever who said, "The world of big business is dividing into those who really have a clear sense of how their business adds some value to society and those who see their sole objective to be purely economic by delivering short-term value to shareholders." It is useful to consider how both of these models have evolved over the years.

THE "MAXIMISE SHAREHOLDER VALUE" MODEL

In the 1970s, many people held Milton Friedman's view that "the business of a business is business." This belief was most established in Anglo-Saxon economies. In this view, social issues were peripheral to the challenges of corporate management. Instead, the sole legitimate purpose of business was to create shareholder value.

---

2 "A Better Deal between Business and Society". *Financial Times*, January 1, 2018. https://www.ft.com/content/94b1eec0-e70c-11e7-8b99-0191e45377ec

The problem with the shareholder value model is that as shown over and over, it blinds management to the important reality that social issues do affect the business. Increasingly due to stakeholder pressure, management is realising that scrutiny and blockages often occur when all stakeholders are not considered in decisions that go beyond creating economic value.

At its core, the shareholder value model lacks Adam Smith's understanding of capitalism as a forceful engine of societal progress. The model that grows business solely for the sake of the business—that doesn't recognise that corporations have a much bigger role than simply enriching shareholders and management—erodes the basic trust between companies and society. Contrast this with Adam Smith's *The Theory of Moral Sentiments*, in which he said that all the members of human society stand in need of each other's assistance and are likewise exposed to mutual injuries. As Smith said, "The wise and virtuous man is at all times willing that his own private interest should be sacrificed to the public interest." Not all leaders in today's business behave as the wise and virtuous man described by Smith.

Over the years, we have seen endless examples of the long-term business impact on social issues. For years, the pharmaceutical sector has been dealing with immense stakeholder activism due to perceived excessive drug pricing. Likewise, the food and beverage industry has been targeted by activists and celebrities to raise awareness of the harmful effects of the sugar content in soft drinks and the links to obesity. A number of countries around the world, including the United Kingdom, have already introduced a sugar tax. Addressing these issues has cost billions of dollars of shareholder value, which could have been prevented if companies had been more aligned with social causes.

The challenge of focusing only on shareholder value is that it can lead managers to exclusively prioritise improving short-term performance, neglecting important longer-term opportunities and issues. Short-term focus has at times resulted in companies compromising ethics and legitimacy.

THE CORPORATE SOCIAL RESPONSIBILITY MODEL

Enter the corporate social responsibility (CSR) model, in which companies undertook initiatives aimed at addressing additional stakeholder relations or that at least made the company look more responsible. CSR practices and departments were implemented across public companies in the mid-1990s and included stakeholder relations, social, environmental and ethical policies relating to the supply chain.

More often than not, the CSR initiatives were treated as separate from the business and were not embedded in the processes, systems and values of the organisation. A slightly cynical view would argue that some businesses adopted CSR practices to avoid scrutiny from NGOs and other activist groups that were threatening the reputation of the organisation.

The challenge of this approach is that too often, companies have used CSR programmes as sticking plasters to obscure more serious shortcomings. Philanthropic budgets that are peripheral to companies' core business models are easy to slough off in a downturn or when conditions become particularly volatile. Sir Howard Davies, former Chairman of the UK Financial Services Authority, once characterised this view as follows: "We carry out our business and, on Friday afternoon, we think about CSR for half an hour." For the most part, CSR and similar programmes are only so much hot air unless they change the behaviour of those in charge of the companies.

THE BIG THREE FORCES IN SOCIETY

The business context has changed significantly over the last years, which has caused these two Social Contract models to become less relevant to the current expectations of society. A renewed thinking is required to ensure that a better relationship between business and society exists.

Before we look at what the new Social Contract should be, we must understand what has changed over the last fifty years and how businesses have responded to these three major forces in society: *Globalisation, Sustainability* and the *Digital Revolution.*

GLOBALISATION

Only a few decades ago, globalisation was considered an unstoppable force by many, and one that promised unprecedented economic growth. The merits of globalisation were promoted by leading world economists and political leaders for years, and society bought into it. Globalisation meant making it cheaper to trade across borders—something that seemed to many at the time to be an unquestionable good. In practice, this often meant that industry would move from rich countries, where labour was expensive, to poor countries, where labour was cheaper. People in the rich countries would be able to retrain and get higher-skilled jobs, and people in poor countries would benefit from employment and economic growth.

The arguments for globalisation rested on the idea that the benefits of a more open and integrated economy would outweigh the downsides. "Freer trade is associated with higher growth… and higher growth is associated with reduced poverty, hence growth reduces poverty" wrote the Columbia University economist Jagdish Bhagwati in his book *In Defense of Globalization.*[3]

Since the 1980s and especially after the collapse of the Soviet Union, lowering barriers to international trade was widely

3 Jagdish Bhagwhati, *In Defense of Globalization* (New York: Oxford University Press, 2004).

accepted by countries all around the world. As a consequence, tariffs were slashed and regulations increased. There was also a sentiment, personified by Margaret Thatcher and Ronald Reagan, that trade unions, which kept wages high and made it harder to fire people, had to be disempowered. In that environment, it was particularly the competition between workers in developing and developed countries that helped reduce wages and job security for workers in developed countries. And while everybody was raving about the merits of globalisation, in 1997, Harvard economist Dani Rodrik published the book *Has Globalization Gone Too Far?*, raising the concern that the cost of greater economic integration would be greater social disintegration.[4] By the end of the 1990s, an activist movement questioning the notion that globalisation was good emerged. This anti-globalisation movement pointed the finger at the highest advocates of globalisation, such as the G7, World Bank and International Monetary Fund (IMF), as well as many flagship businesses, such as McDonald's, Starbucks and Nike. In 1999, a coalition of trade unions and environmentalists shut down the meeting of the World Trade Organization in Seattle.

By the time the Great Recession brought the global economy to its knees, there was no longer a consensus that globalisation was the answer. Previous supporters now agreed that globalisation has produced inequality, unemployment and downward pressure on wages.[5] Globalisation has also multiplied the opportunities for tax avoidance, and tax competition between states has diluted the political will to uphold competition in the marketplace.[6]

4 Dani Rodrick. *Has Globalization Gone Too Far?* (Washington, DC: Peterson Institute for International Economics, 1997).

5 Nikil Saval "Globalisation: The Rise and Fall of an Idea That Swept the World," *The Guardian*. July 14, 2017. https://www.theguardian.com/world/2017/jul/14/globalisation-the-rise-and-fall-of-an-idea-that-swept-the-world

6 Phillip Stephens. How to Save Capitalism from Capitalists," *Financial Times*, September 14, 2016. https://www.ft.com/content/c69e7972-79c0-11e6-97ae-647294649b28

After the recession, the world economy had to deal with the aftermath of the financial crisis, the Eurozone crisis involving the Greek bailout and a sharp decline in the prices of oil and other commodities, which provoked a significant drop in global growth. In the IMF's World Economic Outlook report for October 2017, global growth was projected to rise to 3.6 percent, up from 3.2 percent the previous year, and then increase further to 3.7 percent in 2018. This represented less than half the average of the previous decades.

However, the so-called Asian Tigers (Hong Kong, Singapore, Taiwan and South Korea) benefited greatly from globalisation, as did India and China. The case of China is particularly interesting, as in 1980, China made up barely 2 percent of the world's GDP. Just thirty years later, the country had become the world's second-largest economy, surpassing Japan. During the period from 1990 to 2007, China's urban population more than doubled, growing by nearly 300 million people—most of whom effectively became part of the Western world's labour force. At the same time, per capita income in urban areas tripled.

Ordinarily, increased labour supply in developing countries should result in "significant sections of the population in developed countries experiencing a decline in their living standards as more and more manufacturing and service jobs are outsourced," according to researchers Jagannathan, Kapoor and Schaumburg.[7] But thanks to a combination of factors—including a frugal culture and the lack of a social security system—these new urban Chinese workers saved their earnings instead of spending them. And because the dollar remained the effective reserve currency of the world, their savings flowed straight to the US. "The foreign reserve holdings of US Dollars," Jagannathan, Kapoor and Schaumburg write, "which had been at less than 11 percent of US

7 R. Jagannathan, M. Kapoor and E. Schaumburg, "What Really Spurred the Great Recession," *Kellogg Insight* July 1, 2013. https://insight.kellogg.northwestern.edu/article/what_really_spurred_the_great_recession

GDP prior to 2000, grew rapidly after 2002; in fact they almost doubled over the five-year period from 2002 to 2007."

In hindsight, economists[8] can explain the close correlation between globalisation and the Great Recession of 2008. The massive shifts that globalisation created in the labour supply in developing countries—and the inadequate responses to these shifts—created a seismic imbalance in the global economy that caused the biggest credit crunch ever seen. Technological advances and globalisation sparked a huge and rapid increase in the labour supply from workers in the developing world, especially in China. But without any domestic financial markets capable of absorbing the new wealth these workers generated, large amounts of money flowed into the US. For its part, the US had no controls in place to prevent financial institutions from finding creative new ways to accommodate the influx of cash.

So what are economists saying today? Larry Summers—the prominent American economist, former Vice President of Development Economics and Chief Economist of the World Bank and former Director of the National Economic Council for President Barack Obama—was previously a ferocious advocate of globalisation. Summers now argues that politicians must recognise the "basic responsibility of government is to maximise the welfare of citizens, not to pursue some abstract concept of global good," what he refers to as "responsible nationalism."

Professor Pankaj Ghemawat from New York University's Stern School of Business believes that exaggerated perceptions of globalisation make actual problems harder to solve.[9] Income inequality in the United States, for example, has risen to a level last seen in the 1920s. It is politically expedient to place the blame

---

8 R. Jagannathan, M. Kapoor and E. Schaumburg, "What Really Spurred the Great Recession." *Kellogg Insight* July. July 1, 2013. https://insight.kellogg.northwestern.edu/article/what_really_spurred_the_great_recession

9 Pankaj, Ghemawhat"People Are Angry about Globalization," *Harvard Business Review*, November 4, 2016. https://hbr.org/2016/11/people-are-angry-about-globalization-heres-what-to-do-about-it

abroad, but the limited role of imports in the US economy fits with research suggesting that domestic factors such as technological change and the decline of unions are bigger contributors. In his view, the real solutions for inequality involve domestic policy: taxes, education, labour regulation and so on; by responding by cutting international flows, we distract ourselves from the hard compromises that are really required. On top of that, Ghemawat argues that deglobalisation would depress growth, cutting our capacity to fund more effective policy responses.

The fact is that, whether perception or reality, globalisation is regularly blamed for wrenching job losses in many developed countries, which has caused a division in society. Elections in 2017 in Germany and Austria saw the success of anti-immigrant, anti-globalisation parties that sent a message of hostility to elites and outsiders. In the UK, the same sentiment led to the vote to leave the EU in June 2016.

The question that business, government and civil society faces today is how to help those badly hurt by trade and globalisation. This would involve reinvesting in dislocated communities, providing relocation assistance and encouraging portable health insurance.[10] These are just few of the areas that could bring society and business together to foster growth and shared prosperity.

Certainly, the sentiment has changed; fifteen years ago, British economist John Kay wrote, "Few components of globalisation are inevitable if there is a genuine popular will to stop them. But mostly there is not."[11] The last remark is what has changed most drastically in recent years. Many of the assumptions that were leaned on before for guidance no longer apply. Stakeholder perceptions of issues are not static and the issue of globalisation is a timely reminder.

---

10 G. Pinkus, J. Manyika, S.Ramaswamy. "We Can't Undo Globalization, But We Can Improve It," *Harvard Business Review*, January 2017.

11 John Kay. "The Great Paradox," November 14, 2001, https://www.johnkay.com/2001/11/14/the-great-paradox/.

SUSTAINABILITY

As we will see later in the book, one of the most prominent champions of sustainability has been Unilever, led by Paul Polman. The company's philosophy is clearly expressed by Sue Garrard, Senior Vice President of Sustainable Business Development and Communications at Unilever: "We are very clear that what a company should do is give something back to broader society where it can. Sustainability is at least if not more about the social impact rather than the environmental impact."

Now, let's look at the origins of the sustainability movement and why it became the second largest force in society over the last fifty years. The birth of the sustainability agenda started back in the early '70s, with the initial Earth Summit in Stockholm, Sweden in 1972, which was organised to help define ways to stimulate sustainable development at a global level. Since then, the Earth Summits have been decennial meetings. In 2012, the member states developed the Millennium Development Goals (MDGs). The MDGs included a framework of twenty-one quantifiable targets and sixty indicators to be achieved from 2000 to 2015, which was set up by a consensus of experts from the United Nations Secretariat, the IMF, the Organisation of Economic Co-operation and Development (OECD) and the World Bank.

At the last Earth Summit, called Rio+20, which took place in Rio de Janeiro in 2012, member states decided to launch a process to review progress toward the MDGs and develop a set of Sustainable Development Goals (SDGs), which would build upon the MDGs and converge with the post-2015 development agenda. In 2015, the United Nations General Assembly held the Sustainable Development Summit for the adoption of the post-2015 development agenda.

The SDGs are a collection of seventeen interrelated, global goals set by the United Nations, each with its own targets to achieve. The SDGs cover a broad range of social and economic development issues including poverty, hunger, health, education, climate change, gender equality, water, sanitation, energy, environment and social justice. Also known as "Transforming Our World: the 2030 Agenda for Sustainable Development," or Agenda 2030, the SDGs were meant to replace the MDGs with a new framework that did not distinguish between "developed" and "developing" nations. Instead, the goals apply to all countries.

As soon as the SDGs were launched in September 2015, they caused an avalanche of criticism. *The Economist* called the SDGs "worse than useless," and another commentator referred to them as "a high school wish list on how to save the world."[12] Even Pope Francis in his address to the New York SDG summit in September 2015 warned that countries should not "rest content" with a "bureaucratic exercise of drawing up long lists of good proposals."[13] Bill Easterly, Economics Professor and prominent opinion leader in foreign policy, argues that in contrast with the MDGs, which were precise and measurable, the SDGs are unactionable, unquantifiable and unattainable; he dismissed "ending poverty in all its forms and dimensions," "universal health coverage," and "ending all...preventable deaths before 2030" as rather vague and utopian goals.

Others considered that the key to reaching the seventeen SDGs was to strengthen governance.[14] Sustainable development inherently involves many different stakeholders operating at many different scales, from national governments to transnational corporations to local and international NGOs to small villages. One

12 "The 169 Commandments," *The Economist*, March 29, 2015. https://www.economist.com/leaders/2015/03/26/the-169-commandments

13 William Easterly, "The SDGs Should Stand for Senseless, Dreamy, Garbled," *Foreign Policy*, September 28, 2015. https://foreignpolicy.com/2015/09/28/the-sdgs-are-utopian-and-worthless-mdgs-development-rise-of-the-rest/

14 James Patterson, "3 Challenges Facing the UN's Sustainable Development Goals," *World Economic Forum*, August 4, 2015. https://www.weforum.org/agenda/2015/08/3-challenges-facing-the-uns-sustainable-development-goals/

of the challenges is to get stakeholders working together at the right time and place to solve complex problems. For instance, SDG goal seven—access to affordable, reliable, sustainable and modern energy for all—opens up many complex questions: Who will need to be involved in developing, producing, installing and maintaining the technology and infrastructure to provide universally accessible energy? How do governments, the private sector and communities interact in deciding on appropriate and sustainable energy systems?

A second challenge is how to deal with trade-offs. It's crucial to recognise that difficult choices will also need to be made that may involve winners and losers. For instance, water security could be threatened by decisions to intensify or expand agriculture.

A final key challenge is to ensure responsibility and accountability for progress toward meeting the SDGs. There's a lack of indicators and metrics to evaluate progress on the SDGs. That set of metrics would involve both inputs (i.e., did nation X make the investment to address issues A, B and C?) and outcomes (did we actually achieve our goals to eradicate poverty, improve health, etc.?). There also needs to be a way to use this information to hold responsible stakeholders to account (business sector, NGOs, government and even civil society).

Achieving the SDGs will require national governments, the private sector, the non-profit sector and communities to make decisions based on full commitment to the SDGs. Unless there's a strong willingness and understanding of the implications, the SDGs will fall into the "too complicated to do" basket.

Doug Frantz, Deputy Secretary-General of the OECD, acknowledges that "the reluctance of some business leaders to embrace SDGs is understandable. They worry that the UN is trying to force companies to become charities. They argue that they need to remain focused on returns to shareholders. Government leaders need to take into account the interests of business when they discuss investments." At the same time, he says that "business leaders need to see that SDGs are not just a public good—they are good business. Plenty of data shows that companies that include sustainability in their business plans outperform their peers."[15]

Unilever elaborates further on the effect that responding to society with a sustainability-centred strategy has had on the company. According to Sue Garrard, "SDGs have really helped our employees understand how we're helping the world in some small, modest way. We now have 170,000 people who I think are much more fluid about why they are doing what they are doing."[16]

Regardless of the complexity involved in achieving the SDGs, what is certain is that today, society will no longer stand for some of the damaging practices that were previously tolerated as a part of advancing Big Business.

THE DIGITAL REVOLUTION

The shift from the traditional industry-based economy that stemmed from industrialisation in the twentieth century to an economy based on information technology beginning in the twenty-first century has also transformed the social contract between business and society. This Digital Revolution has created a high-tech global economy and a knowledge-based society, which has transformed every industry and sector and created new industries that didn't exist twenty-five years ago.

One of the most disruptive innovations from the Digital Revolution resulted from the introduction of the internet to all

---

15 Doug Frantz, "The Business Case for the Sustainable Development Goals," *Huffington Post*, March 14, 2017. https://www.huffingtonpost.com/entry/the-business-case-for-the-sustainable-development-goals_us_58c6ffa5e4b034000023f4a47

16 Barry, Mike, Sue Garrard, Joanna Yarrow, Rob Cameron, and Chris Coulter. "Webinar Recap: The 2017 Sustainability Leaders Survey." *GlobeScan*. Webinar. June 28, 2017. https://globescan.com/webinar-recap-the-2017-sustainability-leaders-survey/

parts of business and society. While the initial internet was first deployed in 1969 under the Advanced Research Projects Agency Network (ARPANET),[17] it wasn't until the 1990s that it was privatised and released from the control of the US Department of Commerce. In 1996, the first survey of internet users counted about 40 million; in 2017, it was 3.8 billion, with Asia accounting for the largest number, 1.9 billion. The development and adoption of wireless communication in the early twenty-first century caused a massive growth in subscribers of wireless devices. In 1991, there were about 16 million subscribers to wireless devices, but by 2017, there were 7.5 billion, out of a world population of 7.6 billion.[18] We can safely say that for the first time in history, humankind is connected via digital devices with access to information-exchange networks. These networks allow the production, distribution and use of digitised information, and considering that 95 percent of all information existing on the planet is digitised,[19] this has created a new paradigm regarding how connectivity, privacy and accuracy of information affect businesses.

The expansion of the internet from the mid-1990s onward resulted from the combination of three main factors.[20] One was the technological invention of the World Wide Web by Tim Berners-Lee and his willingness to distribute the source code to improve it through the open-source contributions of a global community of users. Another was the governance of the internet, which kept it under loose management of the global internet community and allowed both commercial and cooperative uses.

---

17 Janet Abbate, *Inventing the Internet* (Cambridge: MIT Press 1999).

18 "Number of Global Mobile/Wireless Subscriptions by Technology from 2010 to 2017 (in millions)," *Statista.* July 2018. https://www.statista.com/statistics/206604/global-wireless-subscription-growth-by-technology-since-2010/

19 M.Hilbert and P.López, "The World's Technological Capacity to Store, Communicate and Compute Information," *Science*, no. 6025. Is 6025. Pg. 60-65 (April 2011). http://science.sciencemag.org/content/332/6025/60

20 Manuel Castells, *The Information Age: Economy, Society and Culture* (Oxford: Blackwell, 1996–2003).

A third factor was the major change in social structure, which prompted behaviours such as networking as a prevalent organisational form, individuation as the main orientation of social behaviour and autonomy as the culture of the network society.

If the dominant cultural trend in our society is the search for autonomy and if the internet powers this search, then we are moving toward a society of assertive individuals in search of cultural freedom, regardless of the barriers of rigid social organisations inherited from the Industrial Age. The implications of this concept are particularly important to understand given that today, we have five different generations in the workplace and engaging them to contribute to the purpose of the company might prove more challenging if the concept of autonomy is not taken into account.

Another interesting force to consider is the evolution from Web 1.0 to Web 2.0 and then Web 3.0 and its implications for the social context. Web 1.0 was the readable phase of the World Wide Web with flat data. In Web 1.0, there was only limited interaction between sites and web users, who passively received information without being given the opportunity to post reviews, comments and feedback. The Web 2.0 phase led to the writable phase of the World Wide Web with interactive data. Web 2.0 facilitated interaction between web users and sites, allowing users to interact more freely with each other and encouraging participation, collaboration and information sharing. Web 2.0 became the social context, and that's when sites like Facebook, LinkedIn and Baidu emerged and took dominant positions. Web 3.0 refers to the executable phase of the Word Wide Web, with dynamic applications, interactive services and machine-to-machine interaction. Web 3.0 is based on a semantic web that can generate and distribute useful content tailored to the needs of users, which is the evolution that many online services have moved toward today. Facebook and many other social platforms tailor the online experience based on the information they have collected about users' online behaviour and preferences.

In the third quarter of 2012, the number of active Facebook users had surpassed 1 billion, making it the first social network ever to do so.[21] As of the third quarter of 2017, Facebook had 2.07 billion monthly active users (those who have logged in to Facebook during the last thirty days).

The key to the success of social networks as societies is that they are not only networks connecting to other networks, or even real people connecting to real people; they are also connected to networks in the offline world. To help understand the context in which businesses operate today, it's important to consider social networks as mini-societies that are all interconnected. It's true that people build networks to be with others they already know or new people with similar interests, beliefs and agendas, but contrary to what critics have said, a social network is not merely a virtual society. Social networks represent a new dimension of the "real world," which, for the first time in history, is characterized by online *and* offline citizenship.

This is a significant paradigm shift for companies and governments around the world. The transformation of communication from mass communication to mass self-communication has created a shift in the landscape of social and political change, by the process of disintermediation of the government and corporate controls over communication. Countless events—such as the Arab Spring of 2010, Brexit, the 2016 US Elections and the rise of populism in Europe in 2016—have all been supported by the cumulative and amplifying power of these networks.

They key takeaway from this change in society is that a genuine understanding of stakeholders must have a real appreciation of how the issues that are driving social change are being rein-

21 "Number of Monthly Active Facebook Users Worldwide as of 2nd Quarter 2008-2018 (in millions)," *Statista*, 2018. https://www.statista.com/statistics/264810/number-of-monthly-active-facebook-users-worldwide/.

forced by the interactions between both the offline society and the online society.

CHEATED AND DIVIDED

To exhaustively sum up the implications of the Big Three Forces in society described above would go far beyond the core purpose of this book. However, it is worth taking a look at the current sentiment in society. Many surveys stress the public's disgruntlement with globalisation and the behaviour of Big Business. A significant part of society also believes that the system is rigged and it's time to throw up the barricades against global capitalism.[22]

For the last seventeen years, the Edelman Trust Barometer has surveyed 33,000 respondents in twenty-eight countries—across different profiles, in the "informed public" category—about their level of trust in business, media, government and NGOs. In 2017, the study found a decline in trust across the board: the average level of trust in all four institutions combined was below 50 percent and the general population did not trust these institutions to "do what is right."[23]

The Edelman study also showed that it wasn't only institutions that suffered from a trust deficit but also their leadership, revealing that "71 percent of survey respondents said government officials are not at all or somewhat credible and 63 percent said the same about CEOs." CEOs were only perceived as credible by 37 percent of global respondents.[24] The most trusted and honest spokespeople are not chief executives but employees.

---

22 Jonathan Derbyshire, "Why Doing the Right Thing Pays Off in Turbulent Times," *Financial Times*, June 2017. https://www.ft.com/content/0c1f39b4-3bb3-11e7-ac89-b01cc67cfeec

23 Matthew Harrington, "People's Trust Has Declined in Business, Media, Government and NGOs," *Harvard Business Review*, January 6 2017. https://hbr.org/2017/01/survey-peoples-trust-has-declined-in-business-media-government-and-ngos

24 Matthew Harrington, "People's Trust Has Declined in Business, Media, Government and NGOs," *Harvard Business Review*, January 6 2017. https://hbr.org/2017/01/survey-peoples-trust-has-declined-in-business-media-government-and-ngos

Examining the reasons for the reported lack of trust, we see that 60 percent of the general population worried about losing their jobs due to the impacts of globalisation, and half said that globalisation is taking society in the wrong direction.

Another study from GlobeScan indicated that nearly seven in ten corporate professionals view social polarisation as a great risk to business.[25] Three areas emerge as being associated with polarisation: instability, greater economic inequality and slowdown and eroding trust.

However, one could argue that this is not a new sentiment. In 2003, Judy Larkin wrote in her book *Strategic Reputation Risk Management*, "The United States and other industrialised societies are currently experiencing some of the lowest levels of confidence in government ever recorded, despite the fact that economic and political conditions have been relatively good in recent years. Trust in government is at an all-time low, characterised by a pervasive decline in deference to authority."[26] The sentiment might have been influenced by the 9/11 terrorist attacks and the collapse of Enron and Arthur Andersen in 2001, in what was one of the biggest corporate scandals in history. Others, like Rupert Younger, Director of the Oxford University Centre for Corporate Reputation, believe that "trust and business have had a very fragile relationship for millennia; look at Shakespeare's *The Merchant of Venice* as an example of distaste for business."[27]

Are things really this bad, or are we victims of reality myopia? In a 2015 survey for YouGov, 65 percent of British people (and 81 percent of French people) said that they thought the world

---

25 "Social Polarisation: A New Risk to Integrate for Business," *GlobeScan*, December 5 2017. https://globescan.com/social-polarisation-new-business-risk/

26 Judy Larkin, *Strategic Reputation Risk Management* (Basingstoke, UK: Palgrave Macmillan, 2003).

27 Michael Skapinker, "Business Will Shrug off Our Loss of Trust," *Financial Times*, November 6 2015. https://www.ft.com/content/334908b2-83b3-11e5-8e80-1574112844fd

was getting worse—but judged according to numerous sensible metrics, they are simply wrong.[28]

If we analyse the development of the world over the last 200 years, we see we have achieved astonishing and remarkable improvements in the quality of life of humankind. For instance, in 1900, worldwide life expectancy was thirty-one years; today, by contrast, it's seventy-one.[29] In 1820, 94 percent of humanity lived in extreme poverty by subsisting on less than two dollars a day in today's value; that fell to 37 percent in 1990 and less than 10 percent in 2015.[30] Every day, 137,000 people around the world move up from extreme poverty. Today, there are about 120 democracies among the world's 193 countries, up from just forty in 1972.

So why do we tend to gravitate toward believing the bad stuff and losing sight of the progress that we have made so far? There are three primary reasons; one is that people are predisposed to thinking that things are worse than they are and they overestimate the likelihood of calamity. This is because they rely not on data but on anecdotal evidence. As we will see in Chapter Eight, this happens not only at an individual level but also at the company level, and it applies to almost every business.

The second reason is that media amplifies distortion. In the digital age, our addiction to bad news just leads us to consume depressing stories across the globe, whether or not they present a real threat to us. This constant consumption reinforces the idea that things are much worse than they are. Furthermore, the constant supply of content in today's 24/7 media is designed to grab the reader's attention, and today's content is less about providing hard facts and more about publishing partisan arguments

28 Steven Pinker, "Is the World Really Better Than Ever?" *The Guardian*, July 28 2017. https://www.theguardian.com/news/2017/jul/28/is-the-world-really-better-than-ever-the-new-optimists

29 Steven Pinker, "Is the World Really Better Than Ever?" *The Guardian*, July 28 2017. https://www.theguardian.com/news/2017/jul/28/is-the-world-really-better-than-ever-the-new-optimists

30 "Better and Better," *The Economist*, September 1 2016.

designed to influence the attitude the reader ought to adopt. All across the media—be it blog posts, opinion columns, books, or TV talking heads—there is increasing competition for our time and it's far easier to seize someone's attention with emotionally charged arguments than mere information.

The third reason why people might not pay that much attention to the positive events around them is simply that improvements might be too remote from their current location and therefore, they might deem the larger trends irrelevant. For example, someone living in one of the most economically deprived areas in the UK might respond to a suggestion that things are getting better with something like, "You are giving me all these facts demonstrating that the world is getting better, but it doesn't feel like that around here." Our focus on the broader picture and the greater good might not be a strong argument to someone who is struggling to make ends meet.

We might be losing sight of the benefits of progress around us, but what is undeniable is that Globalisation, Sustainability and the Digital Revolution have completely transformed the Social Contract and the rules of engagement of that contract.

How can companies build relationships that benefit both parties equally? How can companies be trustworthy and engage authentically? How can companies be relevant to the society they serve? I will do my best to provide the answer to these questions in the following chapters.

CHAPTER TWO

The New Normal

AS WE HAVE SEEN, THE DIGITAL REVOLUTION HAS ALTERED the social dynamic, enabling individuals to connect and form strong networks. This double helix of the "online world" and "offline world" feeds the new social context—"The New Normal." In this chapter, we will examine the three interrelated dimensions that characterise this recent societal shift: Hyper-Transparency, Interconnectivity and Media Anarchy.

Hyper-Transparency allows members of a network to freely share any information. Businesses need to find the balance between what they share with stakeholders and what they aim to keep secret. Hyper-Transparency means that even illegitimately acquired private and confidential information can emerge into the public domain, so any dubious practices or activity can no longer be expected to be contained.

The second dimension, Interconnectivity, is the natural extension of every member of society having the means to communicate with every other via a digital device. Most individuals are no longer confined by geographic and community constraints, which may previously have been the main influence on and output for their values and opinions. We are all now able to disclose and amplify any information based on our cognitive bias and values. This force demonstrates the high degrees of connectivity that are in place to search for and find our social peers in the network that we interact with. These networks are fluid, are constantly evolving and currently extend to over 7.5 billion people around the globe.

The third dimension is Media Anarchy, which has grown from the uprising of unaccredited "writers" or influencers and the proliferation of content-publishing systems across the networks. In tandem with this, the traditional media has fallen into the "publish now, fact-check later" mindset in a bid to stay relevant.

The New Normal has enabled us to strengthen our sense of identity and individuality and as a result, we engage with higher expectations. In this environment, we no longer talk about what is desirable but instead use the language of rights, where every view and opinion is considered to hold the same weight, regardless of the credibility of the source. A disregard for such opinions can quickly trigger claims of exclusion, reinforced by the "echo chamber" created by engaging only with people sharing our views.

HYPER-TRANSPARENCY

Thanks to the ubiquitous nature of information today, there's a level of transparency that is no longer optional; companies can embrace the opportunity to be more direct and transparent, or they can resist change, creating disengagement from key stakeholders. While it is expected that businesses will always maintain a certain degree of privacy, engaging more openly with stakeholders should not be seen as a threat but rather as an opportunity.

Given that today's media platforms act as amplifiers of good behaviour, communication and performance—as well as bad—as BP's former CEO Lord Browne says, "Businesses can turn online transparency to their advantage if they have nothing to hide, if they are willing to have a genuine dialogue and if they have used the proliferation of data without overstepping privacy boundaries."[31]

Driven by the increase in transparency, most companies have changed the way they engage with their stakeholders. Rio Tinto, a global mining company, had to adapt its stakeholder relations strategies in the communities in which the company operates. Simone Niven, Group Executive of Corporate Relations at Rio Tinto shared with me that "society now has much higher expectations, especially of big business, big government and institutions than in the past. We have taken a long, hard look at how we operate. The principles of greater openness and transparency are really changing the way we do our business."

Hyper-Transparency allows for all stakeholders to have the same information and to access that information at all times. Corporations are now more exposed than ever and if an entity is acting in bad faith, the world is likely to find out at some point, whether it be via an employee whistleblowing, unsatisfied customers or a highly scrutinising media.

Hyper-Transparency and the erosion of trust have caused a siloed society with two assumed agendas: good and bad. The good organisations don't feel a need for privacy because they have "nothing to hide," and thus, stakeholders do not fear any secrets being leaked. The "bad" organisations feel a need for privacy, because they "have something to hide" and are fearful of the transparent world. The balancing act is something most companies struggle with today in trying to figure out how to share enough without sharing too much. If and when the public should find out about a corporate "secret" (whether this be positive or negative), it gives the company a negative connotation of secrecy, which damages the trust between the two. Privacy is becoming an unsustainable commodity to rely on, but being completely transparent isn't a viable option, either.

31 John Browne with R.Nuttall and T.Stadlen, *Connect: How Companies Succeed by Engaging Radically with Society* (New York: PublicAffairs, 2015).

Information doesn't fade away after a news story breaks to the general public; customers, shareholders and employees always have access to whatever information is being put online. Today's media tends to focus on the more hyperbolic issues, and it is more likely that many corporations will have a trail of negative coverage in their wake as opposed to the narrative that the company might have tried to present. Hyper-Transparency is becoming almost impossible to ignore; it is how the world has evolved to function and it has become a common thread in society.

Companies need to be proactive and plan for the likelihood that information will emerge into the public domain, whether on their own terms or not. Companies can no longer afford to rely on reactive "reputation management" techniques when a negative story comes to light. The speed with which issues can now escalate means that pre-planned responses, even if never required, are now the sensible approach. Owning the narrative in an authentic manner is fundamental to operating when the world is watching, listening and posting 24/7.

Even when a company is well prepared, being fully transparent with stakeholders can still feel like a risk to many corporate leaders. In the 2014 Cone Communications *Food Issues Trend Tracker*, 55 percent of Americans admitted to not knowing if genetically modified organisms (GMOs) were good or bad for them. With this level of uncertainty around the issue, companies that actively incorporated GMO products in their offerings were reluctant to highlight this practice for fear it would create antagonism within their stakeholder base. However, in the same report, nine out of ten Americans stated it's positive for a company to be transparent about the supply chain as long as it is honest and offers a way to resolve the issue. Stakeholders are more likely to respond positively when the organisation is upfront, honest and transparent; the opposite has a negative effect on the credibility of the organisation.

The Starbucks coffee company is a corporation that has harnessed the skill of initiating dialogue with all stakeholders. Its open online forum "My Starbucks Idea" is a pre-emptive approach designed to give Starbucks a role in the conversation surrounding its brand. Instead of allowing stakeholders to come to their own conclusions on the wildfire of social media, Starbucks essentially created its own platform where all kinds can speak their minds and the company can listen.[32]

Patagonia provides another example of Hyper-Transparency within a brand. On its website, it recommended that customers try and find its products offered for less on websites like eBay. This approach may seem counter-productive, as it would be expected to result in a loss of revenue. However, the initiative highlights the durability of the products while also being aligned with the ethos of sustainability and recycling. So far, it has paid off by forging trusting and meaningful relationships with customers.

The public can't necessarily know everything, though, both on a practical level and for the safety and well-being of the business. Where does one draw the line? While it depends on the corporation, its functions and its products and services, there is no one right answer. There is a substantial difference between protecting privileged information and keeping stakeholders in the dark. The former is vital protection for a brand, while the latter is problematic and can lead to suspicion.[33]

Hyper-Transparency affects all stakeholders: consumers, clients, companies, governments and many more. It also creates a more direct form of communication among all stakeholders. Hyper-Transparency is what led the exposé unveiling the secrets behind Big Pharma pricing and management practices. The most prominent example of this came in 2016, when it was revealed that Mylan had increased the price of its EpiPen 400 percent since

---

32 "My Starbucks Idea." *Starbucks Coffee Company*. 2018. https://ideas.starbucks.com/.

33 Mark Robertson, "Hyper Transparency Global Business," *The Guardian*, February 2, 2015. https://www.theguardian.com/sustainable-business/2015/feb/02/2015-hyper-transparency-global-business

2007 to $550. In May 2015, consumers started tweeting about the increasing prices and by September 2015, *Bloomberg News* began writing articles covering Mylan's staggering revenue increases, though this coverage focused on the success of Mylan's marketing in positioning EpiPen as a must-have device.[34] However, later in July 2016, blogs appeared speculating that the only reason the price was able to increase was due to the monopoly Mylan held on the drug. Later that month, an online petition was started and by August, the speculation was generating up to twenty tweets per day from consumers all over the world. In late August, the petition spread like wildfire, with up to 500 shares a day. Twitter users began tagging politicians, causing the scandal to gain prominence in the mainstream media. On August 23, 2016, the compensation package for Mylan's CEO, Heather Bresch, was made public knowledge and shared on Twitter, which ultimately caused her to testify in front of the United States Senate.

Hyper-Transparency isn't just important for customers; employees also play a crucial role in the matter. Privacy and confidentiality are not the same as they once were; it only takes one Facebook post for the employee of a corporation to blow the whistle on what's going on. An example of employee empowerment came with the multiple scandals that engulfed Wells Fargo in 2016 and 2017, generating vast amounts of media coverage for all the wrong reasons. In a Harris Poll report, Wells Fargo's Reputation Quotient dropped 20.6 points from 2016 to 2017—the biggest drop in the eighteen-year history of the poll. To make matters worse, the Wells Fargo scandal continues to unfold over a year later.[35]

Born out of the gold rush, Wells Fargo has existed since the

---

34 Brad Tuttle, "Why the EpiPen Scandal Sums up Everything We Hate about Big Business and Politics," *Time.* September 21 2016. http://time.com/money/4502891/epipen-pricing-scandal-big-pharma-politics/

35 Gretchen Morgenson, "Wells Fargo Dubbed a Repeat Offender," *The Wall Street Journal*, November 29, 2017. https://www.wsj.com/articles/wells-fargo-is-dubbed-a-repeat-offender-and-faces-new-wrath-from-its-regulator-1511951402

1800s. It has proven itself to be a formidable bank surviving depression, wars, hyperinflation and, more recently, the Great Recession. However, at the height of the recession in October 2008, while Wells Fargo qualified for inclusion in TARP, which aimed to inject capital into the market, it decided instead to raise $25 billion in capital privately. The bank did not want its reputation tarnished and business negatively affected by accepting a loan.[36]

After the recession, Wells Fargo became the "poster child" of big banks and the stock market, reaching a stock price of $69.97 a share in June 2016. The apparent success began to be tarnished when it was revealed that a segment of the bank was pressuring clientele into unnecessary bank accounts and opening accounts under client names without permission. Wells Fargo employees blew the whistle on the malpractice, leading the Consumer Financial Protection Bureau of Los Angeles to fine the bank $185 million on September 8, 2016. As the scandal developed, Wells Fargo fired 5,300 retail employees who had been pressured to meet unrealistic sales goals. It was reported that those former employees had been antagonised by a corporate culture that led to a miserable atmosphere if sales targets were missed and to being fired if they reported illegal practices. For these employees, this was a step too far and they decided to tell the media their side of the story. Wells Fargo's scandal ran so deep, the employees were eager to be the first to come forward.[37]

In 2017, the scandal continued to grow, in both the international and insurance sectors, when it emerged that Wells Fargo's international clients (including Burger King) were overcharged anywhere from 1 to 4 percent on trading fees. The bankers were

---

36 Alan Blinder, *After the Music Stopped* (New York: Penguin, 2013).

37 Emily Glazer, "Wells Fargo, Chasing Bonuses, Overcharged Hundreds of Clients," *The Wall Street Journal*, November 27, 2017. https://www.wsj.com/articles/wells-fargo-is-dubbed-a-repeat-offender-and-faces-new-wrath-from-its-regulator-1511951402

incentivised by a generous bonus policy, and to justify the higher price to clients, Wells Fargo would blame fluctuating exchange rates for any odd charges. To make matters worse, Wells Fargo wasn't faring any better within the consumer market when it was discovered it had charged customers for automobile coverage insurance they didn't need. Twenty thousand customers had their cars wrongly repossessed because they could not keep up with the faulty insurance payments. To some, the bank was perceived as lower on the ethics scale than Big Tobacco.[38]

Following the scandal, Wells Fargo was forced to cut seventy senior-level managers who were involved with the push for false accounts. As a result, Wells Fargo lost its CEO when John Stumpf resigned, while both Stumpf and his successor, Tim Sloan, were called to provide testimony in Washington, DC over the incident. Before the scandal, Wells Fargo was the largest bank in the US, but in 2018, it stands as the nation's third largest bank. In the most recent report from the Office of the Comptroller of the Currency, Wells Fargo's management of compliance risk was characterised as "weak," and in April 2018, Wells Fargo was fined $1 billion for the insurance and mortgage abuses.[39]

Operating in a world of Hyper-transparency is challenging and businesses must adapt to this new reality. When I spoke with Richard Woods, Senior Vice President Corporate Affairs, Capital One, he shared the following: "Few businesses are prepared to operate in an environment of radical transparency, but that's the world we're in. Being prepared means recognizing that every dimension of the company's conduct has the potential to be challenged in some way, by somebody and in public. The goal in managing this risk is not to avoid conflict but, rather, to be prepared to answer

38 Emily Glazer, "Wells Fargo, Chasing Bonuses, Overcharged Hundreds of Clients," *The Wall Street Journal*, November 27, 2017. https://www.wsj.com/articles/wells-fargo-is-dubbed-a-repeat-offender-and-faces-new-wrath-from-its-regulator-1511951402

39 Ben McLannahan, "The Whistleblowers," *Financial Times*, November 7, 2017. https://ig.ft.com/special-reports/whistleblowers/

these challenges quickly and convincingly. This goal is most likely to be achieved when the company acts in advance to eliminate conduct and policies that are inconsistent with its self-declared values, mission or brand promise. Managing your business in a way you feel good about when the bright light of public controversy shines on it is the best way to manage reputation risk. Most companies have within them the institutional knowledge to manage reputation risk proactively. Doing so, however, requires both institutional commitment starting at the top-of-the-house and an efficient process that can bring this knowledge to the fore."

Hyper-Transparency gives stakeholders a new context and increased influence; as a result, businesses end up being highly scrutinised. In the New Normal, if stakeholders are not aligned with what they see, fierce activism is likely to follow.

INTERCONNECTIVITY

Hyper-Transparency may have forced a closer alignment between the business and its stakeholders, but it is Interconnectivity that has tied the threads that join all levels of society to one another. In places where the bond of trust has increased, brand connection and reliance are stronger than ever before.

One of the consequences of Interconnectivity is the rise of collaborative consumption—as consumers continue to trust one another, they begin to consume from one another. This powerful economic phenomenon is reinventing the consumer market through "the coincidence of wants," and this new level of trust has bred websites like SwapTree and Airbnb. Rachel Botsman, an author and lecturer on the "Collaborative Economy," believes that consumers are saying, "I don't want stuff; I want the needs or experiences it fulfils. This is fuelling a massive shift from where usage trumps possessions."[40]

40 Rachel Botsman, "The Currency of the New Economy is Trust," *TEDGlobal*, 2012, https://www.ted.com/talks/rachel_botsman_the_currency_of_the_new_economy_is_trust/up-next.

The interaction of collaborative consumers is making it easier for businesses to receive accurate communication about what stakeholders want. As Alan Zorfas and Daniel Leemon noted, "Shaping a customer experience by being precise about the emotional connections you're trying to build and investing in the touchpoints that drive these connections is a powerful way to increase customer value and maximise the return on investment decisions and minimise the risk."[41]

Another consequence of this increased strength in relations between a company and a stakeholder is that it increases expectations and accountability to keep company promises. The more trust there is, the more there is at stake. Creating deep connections between a brand and its customers is the new face of marketing; loyal customers spread the word, become advocates and are an incredibly useful resource when trying to understand the relationship between the brand and its customers. Today is all about the brand experience and the emotions it creates.

Engaging with customers is a more obvious necessity in the New Normal, but what about society as a whole? What about social movements against injustice or inequality? In 2012, the *Time* 100 list of the most influential people in the world featured Harvey Weinstein as the most powerful man in Hollywood.[42] His reputation for being difficult preceded him for decades. However, with a string of Oscar successes, it appeared that the industry was prepared to put up with his behaviour.

In 2017, this was all to change when allegations of sexual harassment began to emerge.[43] As more and more women came

---

41 D.Leemon, A.Zorfas and S.Magids, "The New Science of Customer Emotion," *Harvard Business Review*, November 2015. https://hbr.org/2015/11/the-new-science-of-customer-emotions

42 Stephanie Abrahams, "Time 100 Confirms the Most Powerful Man in Hollywood," *Time*, April 18, 2012. http://entertainment.time.com/2012/04/18/the-most-powerful-man-in-hollywood/

43 Jonathan Randles, "Weinstein Co. Cuts Deal Price by $23 Million to Close Sale to Lantern," *The Wall Street Journal*, June 22, 2018. https://www.wsj.com/articles/weinstein-co-cuts-deal-price-by-23-million-to-close-sale-to-lantern-1529696308

forward, a picture began to develop of a predator who had been operating for decades, and it was only through Interconnectivity that his accusers were able to create the #MeToo movement that shook up not only Hollywood but also politics and business.

In fact, the #MeToo movement didn't start with Weinstein; it began not in Hollywood but in Silicon Valley. In February 2017, Susan Fowler, at the time an employee at Uber, wrote a blog detailing the sexual harassment taking place at Uber's headquarters. Pulling this one thread caused the whole issue to be amplified quickly and unravelled as victims of sexual harassment from all over the world began to come forward. "Women have been speaking up for many, many years but were very rarely believed, and there were almost never any real consequences for offenders," said Fowler. "This year, that completely changed." Fowler hadn't expected to be at the vanguard of such an influential movement, but her experiences touched a nerve with many around the world.

Fowler's initial post prompted a wave of similar allegations throughout Silicon Valley, and it didn't take long to move its way down the West Coast to Hollywood. Weinstein became the lightning rod for these claims, attracting more interest and coverage than its original source. The scandal broke in October 2017 and it only took about a month for the entire Weinstein Company (which Harvey Weinstein cofounded with his brother) to conclude that selling the corporation had become the only viable option. Profits were lost when reputationally conscious giants like Amazon and Apple cancelled orders of TV series produced by the company.[44] Weinstein had attempted to navigate a way through the storm with a series of different tactics, including apologising, denying the more severe accusations, threatening legal action and admitting himself into a rehabilitation centre for sexual addiction.

44 Jonathan Randles, "Weinstein Co. Avoids Defunct Video Distributor's Bid to Freeze Studio Assets," November 29, 2017. *The Wall Street Journal.* https://www.wsj.com/articles/weinstein-co-avoids-defunct-video-distributors-bid-to-freeze-studio-assets-1511975595

Meanwhile, the company tried to take protective measures by sacking its cofounder, but the incident was just so toxic and sticky that neither could escape the repercussions. Weinstein himself remains ostracised from the industry with more accusations and legal battles mounting up, while his previous company filed for bankruptcy, with its remaining assets auctioned off in May 2018.

The ability of former employees to interconnect with one another caused Harvey Weinstein's reputation to fall to its knees. It didn't stop there however; his interconnectedness with the Weinstein Company also caused the collapse of an entire corporation. The world has arguably never seen a movement of this calibre and it was all done by women on the internet (most of whom have never met face to face). This case demonstrates the potential for Hyper-Transparency to bring an important issue to the fore and for Interconnectivity to both magnify the issue and spread the message to diverse groups of stakeholders who care deeply about the issue.

With Interconnectivity, any scandal has the potential to resonate globally, as demonstrated by the #MeToo movement taking down titans of the Establishment everywhere. In early December 2017, Senator Al Franken stepped down from his position in light of sexual misconduct allegations. John Conyers is another senator who has lost his career amidst the allegations. John Besh, celebrity chef and restaurant owner, also stepped down from his post in his restaurant and other business handlings. These are just a few of the examples of those caught up in a movement that went on to have its most prominent proponents, or "The Silence Breakers," named *Time*'s 2017 Person of the Year.[45]

In the *Financial Times*, Gillian Tett explained that events like this are possible thanks to "digital information cascades" breeding the Interconnectivity strong enough for such behaviour not only

---

45 S.Zacharek, E.Dockterman and H.Edwards, "The Silence Breakers," *Time*, December 18, 2017. http://time.com/time-person-of-the-year-2017-silence-breakers/

to be headline news but also to put its proponents in a state of sustained public shame. The combination of Hyper-Transparency and Interconnectivity has changed the rules of the game, overturning power structures; it has instead provided victims with a sense of almost immediate justice and an active support network. As Tett said, "Executives of all stripes take note: cascades have power."[46]

Interconnectivity has changed the terms between the business and its stakeholders; the transparent, complex way in which society communicates now is both powerful and delicate. Bad news travels faster than ever and once the message is out, it's accessible by almost everybody.

MEDIA ANARCHY

The increased appetite for being up-to-the-minute, the growth in social intrusion and the democratisation and amplification of media outlets have led to the third dimension, Media Anarchy. When I talked with Richard Hamilton, former Director of Corporate Affairs and Strategy at KPMG, he highlighted the risk of Media Anarchy: "Public opinion is the ultimate stakeholder and is alarmingly easily shaped. In an era of social media, those who shout loudest can shape opinions based on their interpretation of the facts, and it's a dangerous concentration of power if a pressure group gets into public consciousness that you have done something wrong, which is an over simplistic explanation of what you have done."

In 2017, The Reuters Institute *Digital News Report* found 54 percent of all respondents with online access use social media as a news source. This was even more prominent in the younger generations, with 33 percent of eighteen- to twenty-four-year-

46 Gillian Tett, "Want to Change the Media? Don't Get Mad—Get Even," *Financial Times*, July 21, 2017. https://www.ft.com/content/2ba2f132-6c18-11e7-bfeb-33fe0c5b7eaa

olds using social media as their main news source, compared with a combined 29 percent who used the more traditional TV or printed newspapers as their main source.[47] As there is so much content fighting for people's attention and social media are often the platform used to consume the news, there has been a shift to delivering shorter snippets of information, with an increasing emphasis on speed and sensationalism over accuracy.

In my conversations with Richard Woods, he shared an interesting insight about the trust attributed to social media channels. "An academic study was conducted at a US university to identify which information channel that would be the most effective in warning students in an emergency situation, such as having an active shooter on campus. It concluded, among other things, that text messaging was far more effective than Twitter for this purpose because students discount a lot of what they read on Twitter. They enjoy Twitter as a source of entertainment but are skeptical about its reliability as a source of credible information."

In today's state of Media Anarchy, the echo chambers of preconceived ideas and beliefs are being reinforced. Furthermore, respected news organisations are side-lining traditional journalistic values in order to fuel the constant demand for new information. Journalism, in its truest sense, is in a downward spiral in the era of instant gratification. With the proliferation of free news and content available online, sales of traditional news outlets have declined sharply. As a result, the industry now has to rely more on advertising to make up for this shortfall in revenue. Advertisers demand a certain number of views, which in turn drives the cycle of shorter, sensationalist and often spurious news stories. Where once the fourth estate—the press—was respected and trusted to educate the public on current events, the industry

---

47 "The 2017 Digital News Report is Now Available." *Reuters Institute/University of Oxford.* June 22, 2017. https://reutersinstitute.politics.ox.ac.uk/risj-review/2017-digital-news-report-now-available

has now fallen victim to a clickbait culture with a "publish now, fact-check later" mentality.[48]

The absence of control, fact-checking and accountability across most online social interactions has left the whole system ripe for abuse. The concept of "fake news" has become so prevalent in the modern psyche that it was named *Collins Dictionary*'s Word of the year in 2017; the publication defined the phenomenon as "false, often sensational, information disseminated under the guise of news."[49] The *Digital News Report* also found that only 24 percent of respondents believed that social media organisations do a good job of separating fact from fiction. Traditional media were still held in higher esteem, with 40 percent believing they did a good job at this, but this is in decline in many regions.

One of the companies most commonly referenced in the fake news debate is Facebook. According to *Statista,* in April 2018, Facebook was by far the most globally used social network, accounting for 17 percent of all active users, while YouTube and WhatsApp were next with 11 percent each.[50] This means that Facebook is one of the largest single distributors of content across the world but without the accuracy, quality control, or reference checking that would previously have been expected of an organisation of this scale.

An additional element of this Media Anarchy came in the form of another shortlisted contender for 2017's "Word of the Year"—the social "echo chamber." Collins defined this as "an environment, especially on a social media site, in which any statement

---

48 Danielle Ryan, "Clickbait Culture and Groupthink Mentality Have Led to the Collapse of Journalism- and the Rise of Donald Trump," *Salon,* January 22, 2017. https://www.salon.com/2017/01/22/clickbait-culture-and-groupthink-mentality-have-led-to-the-collapse-of-journalism-and-the-rise-of-donald-trump/

49 "The Collins Word of the Year 2017 Is...Fake News," *Collins Dictionary,* November 1 2017. https://www.collinsdictionary.com/woty.

50 "Most Famous Social Network Sites Worldwide as of April 2018, Ranked by Number of Active Users (in Millions)," *Statista,* https://www.statista.com/statistics/272014/global-social-networks-ranked-by-number-of-users/

of opinion is likely to be greeted with approval because it will only be read or heard by people who hold similar views."[51] In practice, this means that you are more likely to see content that supports and reinforces your views around the topics of interest rather than be challenged by more neutral or even opposing sources.

When I spoke with Nigel Fairbrass from Eterna Partners, he explained the effect of Media Anarchy in today's business this way: "The collapse in digital publishing costs has afforded anyone with a social media account the same publishing power as a global broadcaster and understandably, people are using this newfound influence to hold organisations to account. Disputes over staff welfare, customer service, product quality, or managerial competence are increasingly played out in a public digital forum, where a company's engagement is scrutinised by a web of interconnected stakeholder groups, moving well beyond the original complainant. These digital channels can be volatile and unpredictable. Emotions aggregate, often at great speed and in our post-factual age, conspiracy theories thrive and are increasingly difficult to check, meaning the credibility of information is dictated as much by how widely it's consumed as it is by any amount of truth."

As we know from the demise of Cambridge Analytica in April 2018 and the follow-up investigation into Facebook's handling of fake news during the 2016 US Presidential Election, the impact of fake news on major political, societal and business issues can be severe.

Alongside the US presidential election of 2016, the most tangible example of fake news in the post-truth world is the Brexit campaign. The Brexit debate thrived on a subtler version of fake news, one that mostly dealt in half-truths, siloed information and warped facts that helped to obscure the larger picture and

51 "The Collins Word of the Year 2017 Is...Fake News," *Collins Dictionary*, November 1 2017. https://www.collinsdictionary.com/woty.

led to a divided nation. The echo-chamber phenomenon was still in effect, with both sides being fed details that supported their position rather than being presented with a balanced overview. The public would be faced with headlines like "Corbyn Confirms Labour Government Would Pay 92 billion Euros in Brexit Bill" when the actual statement from the Labour Party leader was as follows: "Clearly where there are legal obligations on long-term investment projects both in this country and other places that must be adhered to, we must honour them."[52]

Dominic Cummings, Campaign Director of Vote Leave, is credited with having created the official slogan of Vote Leave, "Take back control," and with being the leading strategist of the Brexit campaign. As Campaign Director of Vote Leave, Cummings was questioned and criticised by MPs at the Treasury Select Committee in April 2016 for creating leaflets for the campaign that could mislead members of the public into believing they were created by the NHS. Looking back, 26 percent of all Brexit voters who voted to leave said they were misled by promises made during the campaign.[53] This was the result of the work of a campaign team that knew too well how to use emotional communications to mislead the voters.

There are many examples from the Brexit campaign that illustrate how facts and opinions were manipulated. Some are more complex and their factual accuracy is open to debate, but they have still been presented in a way that was deliberately dividing.

For example, from the Leave campaign:

1. Claim: Brexit will cut immigration massively.

---

52 Andrew Grice, "Fake News Handed Brexiteers the Referendum and Now They Have No Idea What They're Doing," *The Independent*, January 18, 2017. https://www.independent.co.uk/voices/michael-gove-boris-johnson-brexit-eurosceptic-press-theresa-may-a7533806.html

53 Chloe Farand, "Quarter of Brexit Voters Say They Were Misled," *The Independent*, August 22, 2017. https://www.independent.co.uk/news/uk/home-news/brexit-voters-poll-mislead-leave-campaign-nhs-claims-lies-remain-win-second-referendum-a7905786.html

- Truth: This does not consider the fact that the UK was and is still struggling with non-EU immigration.

2. Claim: Brexit will help gain special access to the single market.
    - Truth: To make this economically possible and feasible, the UK will have to keep some sort of immigration movement, depending on the demand for labour.

3. Claim: The UK sends Brussels £350 million per week.
    - Truth: This figure does not include the British rebate or the capital that comes back from EU spending. EU membership cost the UK half that figure in 2015.

From the Remain camp:

1. Claim: The EU is worth £4,300 to every UK household and house prices would fall by 18 percent were the country to leave.
    - Truth: Exact figures like these are hardly meaningful considering they are based on unknown figures and estimates.

2. Claim: As a result of Brexit, EU citizens in Britain and British citizens in the EU will have to return home.
    - Truth: The types of visas and permits needed would have to be negotiated over a span of years, and it is highly unlikely anyone would just be ejected.

3. Claim: Leaving the EU will put 3 million jobs at risk.
    - Truth: This argument was based on a fifteen-year-old estimate of UK jobs that depend on EU exports.

It was clear that in order to win the referendum, campaigners were deliberately targeting and obfuscating the message around a series of preconceived opinions. After votes were counted, Dominic Cummings of Vote Leave admitted as much when he wrote: "Would we have won without immigration? No. Would we have won without [the] NHS? All our research and the close result strongly suggests no. Would we have won by spending our time talking about trade and the single market? No way."[54]

Groupthink made the arguments above easy to believe, depending on a citizen's personal views. Media Anarchy divides society by putting out content that enforces their preconceived opinions, creating an echo chamber of their own warped perceptions. Those presenting the "facts" above were clearly not attempting to present a balanced and nuanced argument; instead, they were clearly driven by a political or even economic motive. These agents used Media Anarchy to manipulate society, rather than providing authentic and trustworthy content that would have informed voters better about the consequences of their decision.

Media Anarchy is not limited to Brexit or Facebook; it could affect any entity at any time. In a polarised society consuming half-truths and with Facebook and other channels amplifying and reinforcing opinions, in the short term, the winner becomes whoever is able to own the narrative with highly emotional claims that touch a nerve in the audience. In the long term, society loses by not being able to hear the truth.

CONNECTED AND TRUSTWORTHY

As we have seen, Hyper-Transparency has made it harder to maintain privacy or hide unethical practices, Interconnectivity allows for information to be shared and propagated faster than ever before and Media Anarchy has made it more difficult to give an accurate account of the facts. These three dimensions are

54 Robert Booth, "Truth Seekers: Inside the UK Election's Fake News War Room," *The Guardian*, January 2, 2018. https://www.theguardian.com/politics/2017/may/19/truth-seekers-inside-the-uk-elections-fake-news-war-room

integral parts of the New Normal driving today's society, and it is fundamental that companies factor in their consequences when establishing the Social Contract.

How can companies establish a healthy and fruitful relationship among stakeholders that creates corporate and societal value?

Businesses that have developed a good Social Contract are those that build social issues into their strategy and business model. The social contract should carry obligations, opportunities and advantages for both sides. We are beginning to see an evolution of the Social Contract away from the Shareholder Value Maximisation or the CSR model described earlier in the book. The new model focuses on making the purpose of the business to maximise the value for society. Research by Harvard Business School Professors John Kotter and James Heskett shows that "purposeful" or value-driven companies have outperformed their peers in stock price by a factor of twelve.[55] Good businesses contribute immensely to society, providing innovations that can transform society in areas related to health, food production, environment, education, employment and prosperity.

Richard Hamilton, former Director of Corporate Affairs and Strategy at KPMG, gave a very clear account of the connection between business and society and why it is fundamental to bring the two closer together when he spoke with me. He said, "I really believe strongly that businesses have to themselves realise that they are part of society, not something separate from it. They might be legally constituted in a way, but they have to act in the interest of shareholders; they have a duty in law to have regard to other stakeholders. It's actually in the law, though most people don't realise; it was added in ten years ago in Section 172 of the Companies Act that a company must have regard to other stakeholders. I believe businesses have to be totally connected

55 J. Kotter and J. Heskett, *Corporate Culture and Performance* (New York: Simon & Schuster, 2011).

with society, and business can only thrive if there is public trust engendered. There will be more business opportunities only if businesses are connected into society and see that they need to act in the way that upholds public trust."

The connected business implements processes to make sure that social issues and emerging social forces are discussed at the highest levels of the organisation as part of overall strategic planning. These are the type of businesses that believe in the value that the role of a "Society Proxy" or Connecting Leader can bring, someone who provides trustworthy intelligence on the impact of stakeholder issues and how these issues affect the performance of the business.

These businesses do not think that their social contract is a "one-way street" that benefits business at society's expense. They understand that they are indeed an integral part of society and as such, they take responsibility for managing these contracts by being more accountable to society's demands, providing more transparent reporting, prioritising the social issues they want to solve, or raising the discussion to work with government to collaboratively find a solution.

Claire Divver, Group Communications Director of BAE Systems, shared the importance of being a purpose-led organisation and how it can drive internal positive change. "Asking questions in the Executive, such as 'Do we believe that what we do is important in the world? Does what we do add value to society?' If that's the case, we must be able to tell the world. Yes, there will be constituents who have a different view, but they will have that view forever unless we put out our side of the story and explain why it's important. A lot of this has come back to purpose. We had to define our purpose in society and [understand] that businesses are not just there to make a profit and supply their customers. They are there to do something of value in the world, and we do something very valuable in the world. That is the thing that most of our employees and our customers value, and that's the thing we want the wider world to understand about the company."

The likes of Colin Mayer of Oxford University's Saïd Business School and *Financial Times* Contributing Editor John Kay both see a "responsible" company as one in which individuals, both management and employees, are seen as members of a group collectively committed to achieving long-term goals. A responsible company understands what Professor Kay calls the "implicit contract" it has with the community to which it belongs.[56] Companies that have this understanding and are built in this way are likely to be more stable and better prepared to deal with economic downturns or stakeholder scrutiny.

According to the essay "Capitalism for the Long Term" by Dominic Barton,[57] there are three elements that can facilitate the improved social contract. First, business and finance must abandon their current short-term orientation and replace it with a focus on long-term value creation. Businesses also need to come to the realization that maximising corporate value and serving the interests of all major stakeholders—employees, customers, investors, suppliers, regulators, media and NGOs—are not mutually exclusive; in fact, research shows the opposite. Finally, public companies need to adopt governance structures in which there is much more accountability and ownership from the boards that govern these companies.

On the first point, abandoning the short-termism that currently limits companies rests on the premise that long-term thinking is essential for long-term success. Barton explains that the long-term perspective adopted by many Asian businesses

56 Jonathan Derbyshire, "Why Doing the Right Thing Pays Off in Turbulent Times," *Financial Times*, June 22, 2017. https://www.ft.com/content/0c1f39b4-3bb3-11e7-ac89-b01cc67cfeec

57 Dominic Barton, "Capitalism for the Long Term," *Harvard Business Review*, March 2011. https://hbr.org/2011/03/capitalism-for-the-long-term

and countries is the reason they have reached the growth and competitive advantage we saw when discussing globalisation.

On the short-term vs long-term debate, it's interesting to note that in 1970, the average holding period for US equities was about seven years, whereas in 2017, it was just four months.[58] This short-term pressure makes it extremely challenging for companies to innovate and take strategic views about issues that affect society. Capital providers such as pension funds, insurance companies and mutual funds must support long-term value creation by allowing businesses to execute their longer-term strategies. Unless the analyst and investor communities change their short-term demands, CEOs will constantly struggle to deliver success based on a long-term plan of corporate value creation.

As we saw earlier in the chapter, maximising shareholder value at the expense of everything else has led businesses to make irrational decisions that have caused the ultimate erosion of shareholder value. Businesses that understand that serving stakeholders is essential to maximising corporate value will offer higher returns than businesses that solely focus on shareholders. Alienating stakeholders in the New Normal can only create disruptive forces that will preclude the business from achieving its goals. Companies no longer operate in isolation and the support of their stakeholders will accelerate their success.

The right ownership structure also has bearing on how the company commits to its social contract. A McKinsey survey in 2010 revealed that the most effective ownership structure tends to combine some exposure in the public markets with a significant, committed, long-term owner. The challenge of many public companies is that no one really owns the place (aside

58 Warren Fiske, "Mark Warner Says Average Holding Time for Stocks Has Fallen to Four Months," *Politifact*, July 6, 2016. https://www.politifact.com/virginia/statements/2016/jul/06/mark-warner/mark-warner-says-average-holding-time-stocks-has-f/

from shareholders) and as a result, boards struggle to perform the single-owner proxy role.

When companies employ board members who spend more time in the business, these board members gain a much better understanding of the business, which can help in supporting the Executive in generating more value across multiple stakeholders. Executive pay also needs to be taken into account to ensure that companies are motivated for the right reasons. Linking compensation to fundamental drivers of long-term value, rather than share price, will encourage a more long-term approach to governance.

Already, change is underway. France and Italy have adopted laws giving longer-term shareholders more control over companies. Environmental, social and governance (ESG) investing is on the rise, with more than half of institutional investments in Europe now taking into account at least one of these factors,[59] while $6.6 trillion in assets in the US are run along these lines. ESG factors probably help shareholders—companies that score well on these measures tend to do well in the longer term.

Larry Fink, CEO of BlackRock, the world's largest asset manager, acknowledged a shift in the debate about the role of business in society in his 2018 annual CEO letter, saying that when "long-term value is created only through long-term investing and stakeholder-centric management, your success will not only be measured in terms of shareholder value return but also in the impact that you're making in society."[60]

There is no doubt that businesses that are fully committed to living by and delivering their Social Contract and that fulfil their obligations will experience less disruption, less intrusion and fewer obstacles from stakeholders, including regulators and

59 John Authers, "Vote of No Confidence in Shareholder Capitalism," *Financial Times*, October 23, 2015. https://www.ft.com/content/c3637524-798e-11e5-933d-efcdc3c11c89

60 Larry Fink. "A Sense of Purpose." *BlackRock*. January 2018. https://www.blackrock.com/corporate/investor-relations/larry-fink-ceo-letter

investors. These are the businesses that have mastered the art of connecting all the pieces to create corporate value and achieve a harmonious balance across all stakeholders. These are businesses that understand how to be relevant in the twenty-first century and the businesses that understand how to be connected to stake-holders by being trustworthy.

CHAPTER THREE

The Authentic Business

IN THE TWO PREVIOUS CHAPTERS, WE EXAMINED THE ROLE of business in society, considered the current environment and explored how the business context has changed, giving more power and choice to stakeholders. As we learned, in the New Normal, stakeholder support comes from being genuinely trustworthy and balancing short-term demands with long-term ambition.

In this chapter, we'll dig deeper into what it means to be trustworthy and what a truly authentic business looks like. Many people are familiar with the marketing version of "authenticity" that is anything but authentic. Our definition of authenticity is less complicated and much easier to spot. We will also look at the complex and often misunderstood concept of reputation and how authentic businesses build their reputations. A good understanding of what drives the company's reputation is necessary to understand the health of the Social Contract.

Simone Niven from Rio Tinto pointed out to us that "we know that trust in business is at an all-time low. The challenge, particularly for multinational businesses, is to figure out how to relate to diverse constituent groups and connect with local people in an authentic way whilst still operating successfully at a global level."

TRYING TOO HARD TO BE AUTHENTIC

Before we dive into the concept of authenticity in its truest sense, let's look at the recent hype surrounding the concept. Over the last decade, "authenticity" has been overused by marketing and business professionals to the extent that it comes across as insincere at best, meaningless at worst.

Consultants tell firms that customers are yearning for authenticity in an age of doubt and mistrust. Indeed, in 2013, the Boston Consulting Group surveyed 2,500 American consumers and found that being authentic was one of the main qualities they said would attract them to a brand. But how can consumers tell when a brand is truly authentic?

Public relations efforts don't make it easy. An article in *The Economist* examines the "authenticity" trend,[61] showing how today's consumer is inundated with a cascade of fascinating facts that strive to bestow a sense of "authenticity" on brands. Even the way companies talk about authenticity can be inauthentic. Interbrand, a consultancy on branding, describes authenticity variously as "internal truth and capability," a "defined heritage," and a "well-grounded value set." What do those phrases mean?

Business leaders have given lip service to authenticity for some time, but the definition remains slippery. A firm called Cohn & Wolfe, for example, has examined the role of authenticity in business since 2012, resulting in a popular rating, the Global Authentic 100. This annual index of global brands is ranked by consumer perception of authenticity. Consumers were asked to rank firms

61 Schumpeter. "It's the Real Thing," *The Economist*, November 14, 2015. https://www.economist.com/business/2015/11/14/its-the-real-thing

on three highly subjective attributes that allegedly define authenticity: reliability, respectfulness and reality. The top five? Amazon, Apple, Microsoft, Google and PayPal.

It looks good to be on that list, but anyone who examines the data closely will realise the results come from only 15,000 consumers of 1,400 brands across fifteen markets. These responses cannot possibly paint a comprehensive picture. Instead, they ring as "PR trying to do PR"—someone created a ranking to develop a story about brands that actually removes the authenticity of authenticity. Carrying out such broad analysis makes it nearly impossible to take into account the cultural norms of the different markets, which raises questions about the validity of the surveys.

What we have learned through repeated cases is that authenticity cannot be faked in the long run and those business that "try hard to be authentic" are found out sooner or later.

A MORE AUTHENTIC DEFINITION

We need a simpler and more universal definition of authenticity. True authenticity means doing what you promise, being consistent in word and deed, demonstrating the same fundamental character in different roles with different stakeholders and being competent in delivering value to your customers and other stakeholders.

We often apply a similar metric at the personal level. A recent article in *The Guardian* confirms this, finding that when we think of the people we most and least admire, authenticity, or lack of it, differentiates those we respect from those we don't.[62] Our estimation of a person might change depending on what they say or don't say, but when people are consistent in their opinions, whatever they are, we respect them. Generally speaking, we admire those who possess self-knowledge, the ability to be honest

62 Stephen Joseph, "Why Being Fake Is Bad for You," *The Guardian*, September 25, 2016. https://www.theguardian.com/lifeandstyle/2016/sep/25/why-being-a-fake-is-bad-for-you

and transparent and a track record of standing up for what they believe in. We don't tend to admire those we see as fake or phony. The same principle applies to business.

The concept of authenticity is universal and timeless. You can't reinvent it; the only way to be authentic is to really be authentic. Johnson & Johnson's authenticity has been tested a few times during its 132-year history. Michael Sneed, Worldwide Vice President of Global Corporate Affairs and Chief Communications Officer, shared with me the importance of being authentic every day, saying, "At truly purpose-driven companies, purpose can't be a set of words or hollow statements, but commitments you really live by every day. Your actions reflect your values, and in today's environment, you will be known by what you do, not what you say. If you live your purpose, you will probably stand the tests of time. If you don't, more and more, consequences will come quickly."

REPUTATION: THE SOCIAL CONTRACT BAROMETER

A positive reputation strengthens market position, reduces the price of capital and increases shareholder value. It can also insulate the brand, allow for higher prices and help to attract the best people. In times when trust is under scrutiny, a positive reputation is well worth having, but it cannot result from manipulation. It must come from the authentic identity of the company.

As we will see in the next chapter, companies like Patagonia that recognise the importance of building an authentic, long-term reputation may wonder how to do it amidst so much marketing and PR confusion about authenticity. How can a company with clearly defined objectives, good character and competence and full awareness of its role in society ensure that it's perceived as it truly is? What does that kind of company look like? How does it form the abstract concept of reputation? To see the path forward, let's look at how society and stakeholders form their perception of any given individual or company.

Countless academic studies and papers have tried to explain reputation and why it matters. In my opinion, the best definition is the simplest: reputation is what others think of you. It manifests based on what you do, what you say and what you achieve. In the business context, reputation is based on the company's behaviour, communication and performance in all areas of the business. Many businesses still believe that reputation is something that can be "managed" separately from the fundamental business, but reputation is not a construct; reputation is an outcome. An authentic reputation evolves from being consistent in word and deed over time. A more helpful way to understand a company's reputation might be to consider it a feedback mechanism of the company's viability and overall performance.

Reputation is itself an outcome, but it needn't be a single outcome; companies have, in fact, multiple reputations. For instance, let's look at the reputation of an oil and gas company through three different stakeholder lenses. The company might have a generally poor reputation for social responsibility in the communities where it operates, it might have a good reputation among shareholders for delivering healthy returns, and employees might feel equally positive about the company for providing a good employee experience. Each of the three stakeholder groups will assess the health of the relationship with the oil company based on a different set of personal expectations, which will result in different reputations. Reputation is in the eye of the stakeholder, and all companies have multiple stakeholders.

For many years, there's been a debate over who owns the reputation of the company. Is it Corporate Affairs or the Communications team? Is it the CEO? Is it the whole company? In our conversation, Michael Sneed of Johnson & Johnson shared his view: "We look at our reputation as an endowment that we collectively want to build over time. In our Global Corporate Affairs organization and global communications organization, we go to great lengths to ensure our partners understand that reputation is something we all own together. As a result, we find ourselves frequently facilitating conversations as various business leaders weigh decisions that could either positively or negatively affect our reputation. In this sense, we play a role of counselor and expert, but ownership is ultimately shared. This works well. It means our partners are more likely to seek our input when the company is at risk, and more likely to share success stories with us so that we can leverage them to the benefit of the reputation of the overall enterprise."

HOW AUTHENTIC REPUTATIONS ARE FORMED

Authentic connection with stakeholders can only happen when the engagement is based on the company's true identity, which, as Professor Grahame R. Dowling puts it in his book *Winning the Reputation Game*,[63] manifests in the company's objectives, character and competence. These three components are in turn manifested in the company's communication, behaviour and performance, thus forming the multiple reputations of the company. Authentic reputations need to emerge naturally from the company's identity before any other tactics will work. As we will see throughout this book, companies that are more "connected" and embed reputation in their identity are likely to acquire a stronger reputation, and the goodwill of those relationships can help to provide a support base in difficult times.

According to Richard Woods from Capital One, strong reputations are supported by two pillars: "Pillar number one is becoming famous for something compelling. Pillar number two

63 Grahame R. Dowling, *Winning the Reputation Game: Creating Stakeholder Value and Competitive Advantage* (MIT Press, 2016).

is managing risk to the company's reputation. Companies need strategies to ensure that they become well-known for the great things they're doing but don't become infamous for the other choices they make along the way."

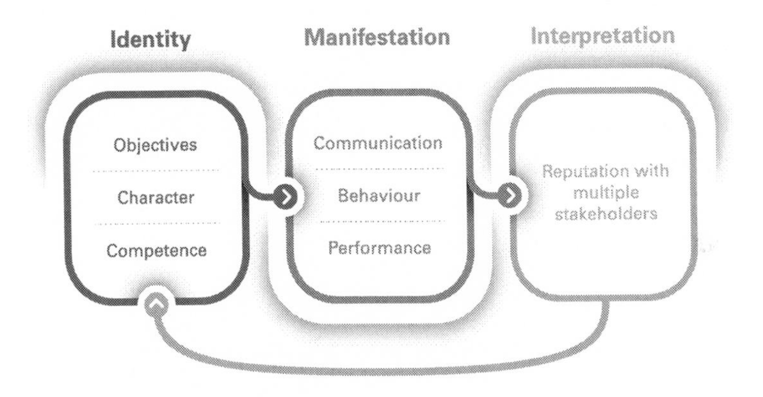

AUTHENTICITY COMES FROM YOUR IDENTITY

Understanding the company's identity will help the company understand what it can and can't do and how to achieve agility and authenticity in a changing world. Identity is not to be confused with the DNA, although at times, it's used to imply the same concept. We know from biology that DNA contains the instructions an organism needs to develop, function and reproduce. It is formed at conception and does not change. However, the same DNA can express itself in different ways based on one's environment. Sue Garrard from Unilever sees the benefit of being aligned with the DNA. She says that "the more your work is tuned in with the DNA of the business, the easier it is to drive change."

Let's take a look now at the three components that define the company's identity: Objectives, Character and Competence.

OBJECTIVES

How the company balances the tension between profits and how it adheres to a set of social and environmental goals[64] will determine what type of company it will become. Under this criterion, we have defined three types of companies, which we will examine in detail in Chapter Four:

- Profit First companies are those that put profits before any social principles.
- Profit & Society companies make profits as well as achieving their sustainability targets.
- Society First companies put profits after their chosen social principles.

In today's business sector, we frequently find companies deploying resources on a large scale without any clear notion of what their purpose is. The objectives and strategy have no connection with any other purpose beyond creating economic value. Robin Nuttall, a partner at McKinsey and co-author of the book *Connect*, highlighted in our conversation that "the first objective is [to] define a purpose which is clear but also which is bold; [purpose] is the most important driver of performance rather than a feel-good factor where no one is really sure what they're doing." Companies must be clear about the role of the business in society and align objectives and strategy with the pursuit of the authentic purpose, thus becoming better connected.

CHARACTER

Character is the second component of the company's identity, which can be found in its vision, mission, ethics, credo and values.

64 Grahame R. Dowling, *Winning the Reputation Game: Creating Stakeholder Value and Competitive Advantage* (MIT Press, 2016).

These are the behavioural norms of the company, or "the way things are done here." According to Ron Carucci, cofounder and managing partner at Navalent, employees want their company's values to be sacrosanct.[65] When they aren't, the logical conclusion workers draw is that the organisation doesn't mean what it says—and that it's perfectly acceptable to behave in ways that contradict the stated values.

The painful result of widespread misuse of company values, according to one major study, is that only 23 percent of US employees strongly agree that they can apply their organisation's values to their work every day and only 27 percent "believe in" their organisation's values. Another comprehensive study based on more than 1,000 firms on the Great Place to Work list reveals a strong correlation between a company's financial performance and the extent to which employees believe their company's espoused values are practised.[66] Values hold the power to drive meaningful differences in performance by shaping a culture, and when misused, can undermine its performance with toxic force.

True cultural norms drive results and engender strong communal pride. Culture in such companies becomes a competitive advantage that attracts top talent and must reflect what makes it uniquely successful, conveying to employees, "This is what it takes to succeed here." Processes like strategy, selection, rewards, performance management and resource allocation must have values woven deeply into them with undeniable consistency between actions and words.

While mission statements are widely misused in businesses today, we can find a handful of companies that have used them successfully by embedding the strong values that have guided their

65 Ron Carucci, "How Corporate Values Get Hijacked and Misused," *Harvard Business Review*, May 29, 2017. https://hbr.org/2017/05/how-corporate-values-get-hijacked-and-misused

66 Ron Carucci, "How Corporate Values Get Hijacked and Misused," *Harvard Business Review*, May 29, 2017. https://hbr.org/2017/05/how-corporate-values-get-hijacked-and-misused

decision-making, and helped them flourish over more than a century. An example of such companies is Johnson & Johnson. Before it went public in 1943—fifty-seven years after it was founded—Robert Wood Johnson, chairman from 1932 to 1963 and a member of the company's founding family, crafted the company's Credo:[67]

> We believe our first responsibility is to the doctors, nurses and patients, to mothers and fathers and all others who use our products and services. In meeting their needs, everything we do must be of high quality. We must constantly strive to reduce our costs in order to maintain reasonable prices. Customers' orders must be serviced promptly and accurately. Our suppliers and distributors must have an opportunity to make a fair profit.
>
> We are responsible to our employees, the men and women who work with us throughout the world. Everyone must be considered as an individual. We must respect their dignity and recognize their merit. They must have a sense of security in their jobs. Compensation must be fair and adequate and working conditions clean, orderly and safe. We must be mindful of ways to help our employees fulfil their family responsibilities. Employees must feel free to make suggestions and complaints. There must be equal opportunity for employment, development and advancement for those qualified. We must provide competent management and their actions must be just and ethical.
>
> We are responsible to the communities in which we live and work and to the world community as well. We must be good citizens—support good works and charities and bear our fair share of taxes. We must encourage civic improvements and better health and education. We must maintain in good order the property we are privileged to use, protecting the environment and natural resources.

67 "Our Credo," *Johnson & Johnson*. 2013. https://www.jnj.com/about-jnj/jnj-credo.

> Our final responsibility is to our stockholders. Business must make a sound profit. We must experiment with new ideas. Research must be carried on, innovative programs developed and mistakes paid for. New equipment must be purchased, new facilities provided and new products launched. Reserves must be created to provide for adverse times. When we operate according to these principles, the stockholders should realize a fair return.

Michael Sneed shared more context about the Credo, how it is being used within Johnson & Johnson and the impact the Credo has had in the success of the company over the last hundred and thirty-two years:

> At Johnson & Johnson, we believe our reputation, trust, and growth are all interconnected. This is why Our Credo represents the foundation of our operating plan and strategic framework. We truly do believe that if we meet the obligations set forward in each of the paragraphs of Our Credo, we will grow and perform in a positive manner. We will deliver for our customers in a way nobody else can. We'll be satisfying employees in terms of both personal and professional growth. We'll be known as a great partner in our communities, and our shareholders are going to receive an outstanding return and continue to invest in our organization.
>
> The purpose of our Corporate Affairs team is truly, first and foremost, to drive the growth of Johnson & Johnson by protecting our overall reputation. We want to take everything we are doing to deliver on the commitments of Our Credo and ensure that wherever you are in the world, if you are engaged with Johnson & Johnson in any capacity, you have a strong idea of who we are and what we stand for. If we do this successfully, we believe we will have employees who are engaged and delivering on our purpose, partners who want to work with us to develop future innovations, and trust in communities so

that we can work together to solve society's biggest healthcare challenges. Taking that commitment seriously truly is our path to growth.

COMPETENCE

Competence is the final component of the company's identity, which is made up of a cluster of related abilities, commitments, knowledge and skills that enable an organisation to act effectively in a job or situation. Competence indicates sufficiency of knowledge and skills that enable the business to deliver in line with stakeholders' expectations, and will vary from company to company.

In order to build the identity that will lead to an authentic reputation, each of these elements needs the same attention. A company will appear untrustworthy in the long run if it is not behaving in line with social norms, even if it's being very competent in its business and achieving significant profits.

STRATEGIC STAKEHOLDERS

Ultimately, how your stakeholders perceive your company will form your reputation. You will be judged on three elements: behaviour, communication and performance. How do you behave with your stakeholders? How do you communicate with them? And finally, do you achieve the objectives you have set out to achieve?

Stakeholders, either through direct contact with the business or via channels of amplification (all forms of media) receive information on each of these three dimensions, which ultimately are "processed" by the stakeholder to form a perception of the company. In the New Normal, this happens 24/7.

The final step to understanding reputation is to identify which stakeholders matter the most to the company. It is key to build healthy and balanced relationships with the company's stakeholders, as ultimately, reputation is determined by how well a company meets the stakeholders' demands in its everyday business activities.

However, it's unrealistic and probably inauthentic to "be all things to all people." Taking into account the company's identity, the company must identify which are the primary and most impactful stakeholders, i.e., the ones that the company will be investing reasonable resources to engage with.

Academic research shows that stakeholder prioritisation should be based on three stakeholder features: Power, Legitimacy and Urgency. Power refers to the extent to which the stakeholder has the influence to impose their will with the company or gain access to a network of influencers who will exercise enormous pressure on the company. Legitimacy happens when the stakeholder actions toward the company are appropriate within the norms, values and beliefs of the larger society. Finally, Urgency is the extent to which stakeholder efforts call for immediate action by the company.

Capital One established a similar stakeholder identification model. According to Richard Woods:

> Bank stakeholders form three concentric circles of importance and urgency. At the center are customers, employees and investors. It pays to invest a lot of time and money to get things right for them. The second circle is comprised of regulators, community groups and media influencers. They are important constituencies but, to a significant degree, the risks with them are an outcome of performance with the first circle of customers, employees and investors. The third and final circle includes elected officials. Persistent failure to meet expectations of fair play, especially among customers, could lead to significant push back from elected officials. Financial industry reform legislation launched as a consequence of the Great Recession is a case in point.

WOLF IN SHEEP'S CLOTHING

In contrast to the reputations that naturally emerge from the identity of the organisation are those that are created around communications campaigns *disconnected* from the core of the organisation. These efforts can be seen as superficial rather than a genuine attempt to be authentic; consumers and other stakeholders have become increasingly suspicious of spin. At the opposite end of the spectrum from companies that build authentic reputations, we find the "dark arts" that some PR professionals have used over the years, which only add to society's mistrust of and discontent toward business.

The "Reputation Management" sector flourished over the last twenty-five years based on the false belief that reputation is a construct that can be created by spin doctors and public relations professionals with the aid of press releases, lobbying and social influencers. While it would be unfair to paint all PR advisers with the same brush, the PR sector has contributed to confusion among senior business executives who struggle to understand how reputations are formed and measured. As we have seen, reputations are built on a foundation not only of communications but also of deeds: stakeholders can see through PR that is not supported by authentic and consistent business activity. Consumers, according to research from McKinsey, feel that companies rely too much on lobbying and PR unsupported by action. If companies rely on PR alone with little insight into the root causes of reputational problems, responses to reputational challenges become short-term, ad hoc and defensive.

As Lauren Day, CCO of Prudential Financial, told me, "The PR profession has a PR problem. How many of you have noticed that the communicators portrayed in the media, in the movies, are spin doctors in the most negative sense? Spinning the news, protecting an unpopular figure, covering up scandals, distorting the truth, contributing to a zeitgeist of distrust and antagonism.

'She's in PR' is sometimes almost a pejorative. The lack of prestige is contributing to a talent gap. Why does the best talent today make the choice to enter other fields of work, in other sectors?"

The concept of reputation deserves better understanding and treatment from some PR agencies. Traditional spin is the completely wrong way to deal with the stakeholder concerns that are exposed in the current media landscape. As we have seen in this chapter, trustworthiness depends upon successful relationships inside and outside the organisation, relationships that are based on authenticity. Spin completely removes any chance to create the binding trust between the company and its stakeholders.

A professional services advisory firm relies much more on the trust placed on the members of the firm than traditional businesses where the reputation is also built on the quality of the product or service. For legal, accounting, management consulting, or PR, there should be no room for unethical or irresponsible practices, let alone advice that would induce the client to behave unethically. Arthur Andersen disappeared overnight following its involvement with Enron, and Bell Pottinger went into receivership after the PR firm worked on the controversial campaign for Oakbay, a company owned by the wealthy Guptas family in South Africa.

Some agencies are contributing positively by bringing academic rigour to their practices, a move welcomed by corporate practitioners. A clear example is the work of Rupert Younger, Founding Partner at Finsbury, who in 2010 set up the Centre for Corporate Reputation at Oxford University's Saïd Business School. The Centre has become a leading body for academics, practitioners and vendors to learn about and research how corporations and institutions create, sustain, destroy and rebuild reputation.

Furthermore, there have been recent calls by prominent PR professionals to bring a more robust approach to PR ethics standards. In October 2017, following the Bell Pottinger case, Richard Edelman, Founder and President of global agency Edelman, characterised the current industry regulations as "a crazy quilt of PR standards," proposing a four-part PR Compact whereby PR professionals must insist on accuracy, demand transparency from clients, engage in the free and open exchange of ideas and require all staffers to take a free universal ethics training course online.

Authentic business must carry out the necessary due diligence when choosing the agency, as any agency that has a compromised ethical code would create a reputation spillover into the reputation of the company.

For any company that makes possessing a value-creating reputation a strategic imperative, it's fundamental to understand that kind of reputation emanates principally from being authentic (true to your identity) and from being Connected with all your key strategic stakeholders. In this chapter, we have covered what it means to be authentic. In Part Two, we will present a model to Connect with the company's constituents, including society—but first, let's look at the role that profit plays in the company's identity.

CHAPTER FOUR

Profit vs Society

AS WE SAW IN THE PREVIOUS CHAPTER, THE RELATIONSHIP that the company has with profits determines the identity of the organisation, which in turn determines the Social Contract. In this chapter, we will present one company for each category: Apple as Profit First, Unilever as Profit & Society and Patagonia as Society First.

All of these companies are highly successful, have developed a very distinctive identity and are seen as business pioneers. However, as we will see, each of the companies has adopted a different relationship to profit, which has shaped their respective roles in society.

PROFIT FIRST: APPLE

Profit First companies are just what they sound like—companies whose first priority is making a profit and the creation of economic value; however, some try to do this without neglecting their social responsibility.

The "poster child" of the Profit First category is Apple. In May 2018, Apple's market capitalisation was $935 billion (more than the entire GDP of Turkey), making it the most valuable public company ever. Apple's reputation for producing great products is excellent. In 2017, Apple topped *Forbes*'s annual study of the most valuable brands in the world for the seventh straight year, at a worth of $170 billion. Its brand value was up 10 percent over the previous year. The secret is in being simply better that the competition in every sense and in reflecting authenticity in everything it does. Apple's history teaches many valuable lessons, not only from Steve Jobs but also from its current CEO, Tim Cook.

"THINK DIFFERENT"

Consider Jobs's actions back in 1997, when Apple was in deep trouble. It reported only $69 million in first-quarter revenue and was forced to lay off 30 percent of the workforce of 13,400.[68] (Apple survived because of a $150 million investment from Microsoft that helped Apple keep its operating system viable and avoid monopoly antitrust concerns.)[69] Steve Jobs firmly believed that Apple could create major innovation breakthroughs that would reshape future industries. He also recognised that the company needed to embed innovation in its identity as a competitive advantage. Shortly after re-joining Apple in 1997, in a meeting with Apple's top executives, Jobs infamously roared, "The products SUCK! There's no SEX in them anymore."[70] Shortly after that, the company began leveraging industrial design to produce more aesthetically pleasing products. Jobs almost instantly revitalised Apple's image by pushing the limits of technology and design,

---

68 John Markoff, "Apple to Trim Jobs and Its Product Line," *The New York Times*, March 15, 1997. https://www.nytimes.com/1997/03/15/business/apple-to-trim-jobs-and-its-product-line.html

69 Roben Farzad, "Microsoft's Apple Investment: The Worst Deal of Them All?" *Bloomberg*, December 10, 2013. https://www.bloomberg.com/news/articles/2013-12-09/worst-deal-ever-microsofts-apple-investment

70 "Steve Jobs's Magic Kingdom: How Apple's Demanding Visionary Will Shake Up Disney and the World of Entertainment," *Bloomberg Businessweek*, February 6, 2006. https://www.bloomberg.com/news/articles/2006-02-05/steve-jobs-magic-kingdom

because that's what Apple was all about. The appointment of Jonny Ive as head of Apple's in-house Industrial Design group was instrumental in elevating the products to what they are today, beautiful and easy-to-use technology devices that have become central to our daily lives.

Apple also launched its "Think Different" campaign in 1997. The television advertisements featured major artists, scientists and politicians who were seen as independent thinkers and icons of our time, including Albert Einstein, Martin Luther King Jr, John Lennon, Thomas Edison, Amelia Earhart, Alfred Hitchcock, Pablo Picasso and Jerry Seinfeld. Apple's advertisements had less to do with specific products and everything to do with the company's ethos.

Apple created the unique culture that came to define Silicon Valley's hard-working but relaxed and casual atmosphere. Working at Apple was hailed as "less of a job, more of a calling." Apple looked for employees who were on a mission to "change the world" and create "some of the best-loved technology on the planet." Apple promoted employment to prospective candidates as "a whole different thing—corporate jobs without the corporate part." Apple looked for people who were "smart, creative, up for any challenge and incredibly excited about what they do. In other words, Apple people. You know, the kind of people you'd want to hang around with anyway."[71] From the start, Steve Jobs had been more than instrumental in developing Apple's envied corporate culture. Employees typically worked sixty to seventy hours a week and no one complained.[72]

Jobs was the ultimate example of an "I'm a genius and I don't care" attitude. Apple employees embraced their hero and became convinced that, with confidence and creativity, they, too, could

71 "Jobs at Apple,". *Apple.* 2018. https://www.apple.com/jobs/us/.

72 Frank T. Rothaermel, *Apple Inc. Case Study* (McGraw-Hill Education, 2015).

become rich and leave a legacy. But Apple understood that it had to stand for something and it could not be afraid to tell the world what that was. From the beginning, Steve Jobs created a culture where he was uncompromising about excellence and where the higher purpose of the business would prevail above everything else.

THE CULT OF APPLE

Apple's rebel spirit not only attracted a long-lasting appreciation from loyal employees but also created a cult-like following among customers who appreciated Apple's propensity to think differently. Millions of people wanted to be seen as unique individuals and hence, millions of people bought Apple products. There was even a "Cult of Apple," a group of rumoured fanatical followers devoted to all things Apple. "While there are many customers who eat, think and breathe Apple, members of the Cult of Apple take their devotion one step further and *believe* in Apple."[73]

The result was that Apple had a conspicuous horde-like following walking down the streets of every major city in the world with the company's signature white earbuds attached to their heads. Apple products became so trendy that other companies had to design their consumer electronics like Apple's to have any hope of selling. The loyalty of Apple customers has served the company well and now it is not just the diehard fanatics who believe.[74]

The one competency that kept Apple on the cutting edge, all the way from start-up to survival and success, has been innovation that others envy. "Innovation distinguishes between a leader

---

73 "1999 APPLE AND MICROSOFT: JOBS BAREFOOT UNDER A TREE." *The Free Library*. January, 26 1996, https://www.thefreelibrary.com/APPLE AND MICROSOFT: JOBS BAREFOOT UNDER A TREE.-a053999515

74 Frank T. Rothaermel, *Apple Inc. Case Study* (McGraw-Hill Education, 2015).

and a follower," Jobs repeatedly said. Jobs believed that innovation is a process that can be cultivated and managed within an organisation, through effective leadership and a supportive culture embedded in the identity of the company.

THE COOK DOCTRINE

When Steve Jobs passed away in 2011, many feared the company would lose its trajectory. Nothing could be further from the truth. Successor Tim Cook has not only kept Apple alive but also taken it to record performance every year. That was only possible because Apple was so clear about its role in society: to change the world and create some of the best-loved technology on the planet. It didn't change when the torch was passed from one leader to another.

In fact, Cook handled the transition masterfully from the start. One week after Steve Jobs announced plans to go on his first medical leave of absence from Apple in 2009, Cook had to answer to Wall Street. He joined two other Apple executives for Apple's quarterly earnings call and was greeted, unsurprisingly, by questions about Jobs's health and the likelihood that Cook "would be the candidate" to take over as CEO if Jobs were unable to return. Another executive on the call offered a quick boilerplate response to the question, but then Cook chimed in with a brief monologue that some later dubbed the Cook Doctrine:

> There is extraordinary breadth and depth and tenure among the Apple executive team...And the values of our company are extremely well entrenched. We are constantly focusing on innovating. We believe in the simple, not the complex. We believe that we need to own and control the primary technologies behind the products that we make and participate only in markets where we can make a significant contribution.

> We believe in saying no to thousands of projects, so that we can really focus on the few that are truly important and meaningful to us. We believe in deep collaboration and cross-pollination of our groups, which allow us to innovate in a way that others cannot. And frankly, we don't settle for anything less than excellence in every group in the company and we have the self-honesty to admit when we're wrong and the courage to change. And I think regardless of who is in what job those values are so embedded in this company that Apple will do extremely well.[75]

He didn't talk about profits. He didn't talk about performance. He was disclosing the identity of Apple. If those values weren't already in place, he couldn't have said any of it without tarnishing his credibility or his ability to follow Steve Jobs. It wasn't manipulation or smoke and mirrors. It was about reinforcing the company's identity, which it would maintain regardless of Steve Jobs or any other individual at the helm. After that earnings call, analysts and journalists began praising Cook for having a clear understanding of Apple's identity and how to run the company with or without Jobs.

Since Cook took over as permanent CEO, an evolution of the doctrine has emerged through his public statements as well as his actions at the company, indicating that he is working to tweak that identity for the better. Cook himself was authentic from the start; he made it clear he wasn't trying to replicate Steve Jobs's role. Instead, he has played his own role using his own style within the culture of Apple and because of that, he has gained a lot of respect.

---

75 Seth Fiegerman, "Tim Cook's Philosophy at Apple, in His Own Words," *Mashable*, September 17, 2014. https://mashable.com/2014/09/17/tim-cooks-apple/#yUf9LH4iGsq4

Some of the most noticeable strategic wins:

- The power of collaboration.

  When Apple announced the big executive shakeup in 2012 that pushed out then-iOS Chief Scott Forstall, the company framed the move as an effort to "encourage even more collaboration between the company's world-class hardware, software and services teams." Although the statement may have been a PR spin on a messy situation, using the word "collaboration" was a meaningful choice and one that Cook has repeated, because it represents a key part of his philosophy in running Apple.

- Inclusion inspires innovation.

  In his office at Apple, Tim Cook displays pictures of Robert F. Kennedy and Martin Luther King Jr. The pictures tie into his deeply held convictions regarding civil rights. When asked to describe his most important values personally, he listed off the following: "Treating people with dignity. Treating people the same. That everyone deserves a basic level of human rights regardless of their colour, regardless of their religion, regardless of their sexual orientation, regardless of their gender. That everyone deserves respect. I'll fight for it until my toes point up."

- Improve the world, not just the margins.

  "We want to leave the world better than we found it," Tim Cook has said.[76] It's a sentiment Cook has expressed several times and one that explains his visible excitement for Apple's attempts to improve education with the iPad. Under Cook's leadership, Apple has started matching employees' charitable contributions; it has pushed for 100 percent renewable energy at some of its data centres and its new

76 Luke Edwards, "Tim Cook: 'We Want to Leave the World Better than we Found It,'" *Pocket-lint*, April 22, 2014. https://www.pocket-lint.com/gadgets/news/apple/128546-tim-cook-we-want-to-leave-the-world-better-than-we-found-it-apple-offers-free-product-recycling

headquarters; and it has worked to improve conditions in its supply chain, which continues to be a thorny issue for the company. (The *Financial Times* reported six high school students claimed they routinely worked eleven-hour days assembling the iPhone X, which constitutes illegal overtime for student interns under Chinese law.)[77]

- Pay attention to Wall Street.
  Cook has repeatedly displayed more of a concern for Wall Street than his predecessor. He has taken more time to meet with investors, presided over massive stock buybacks and even tied some of his bonus to Apple's stock performance.

- Be more transparent about corporate issues, more secretive about products.
  "Apple" and "transparency" weren't traditionally words people put next to one another, but Cook has made it a point to change that—at least when it comes to issues involving the company's supply chain, environmental efforts and other corporate affairs.

THE THORNY ISSUES

Apple is a perfect example of how to build an authentic corporate reputation as a Profit First company. Its contribution to society and human progress, while not measured in sustainability metrics or philanthropic efforts, is second to none and goes far beyond the economic value.

However, despite its indisputable success, Apple has faced a number of issues over the years involving tax avoidance and supply chain working conditions. In 2016, the European Commission issued a $15 billion tax penalty over illegal Irish aid and in 2017, with the publication of the Paradise Papers, found that

77 Yuan Yang, "Apple's iPhone X Assembled by Illegal Student Labour", *Financial Times*, November 21, 2017. https://www.ft.com/content/7cb56786-cda1-11e7-b781-794ce08b24dc

Apple was allegedly sheltering $250 billion in tax havens on Jersey, in the Channel Islands. Offshore working conditions have also been questioned over the years, such as the exploitation of Chinese workers at Foxconn, which employs an estimated 1.2 million employees to assemble Apple products. These issues have dented Apple's reputation.

As a result, the company has made an effort to take control of its issues by being more transparent. It has issued a paper explaining its tax strategy as well as providing extensive information on its efforts to audit supply chain working conditions.

In the New Normal, no public organisation is free from public inspection, and when you are the most valuable company in the world, you are especially likely to receive the most intense scrutiny. What's important for stakeholders is maintenance of the values that have made the company so terribly successful. In the words of Tim Cook, Apple has the "self-honesty to admit when we're wrong and the courage to change."

THE NEXT FRONTIER

The past decade has seen the smartphone become a portal for managing daily life—consumers use it to bank, buy and befriend. How can Apple continue delivering great economic results while being aligned with Steve Jobs's original, personal ethos: "to make a contribution to the world by making tools for the mind that advance humankind."

Apple has spent three years preparing its devices and software to process medical data, offering products to researchers and clinical-care teams. On January 2018, it announced the next big software update for its iPhone included a new feature, Health Records, to allow users to view, manage and share their medical records. Embedded in Apple's Health app, the new feature brought together medical data from participating hospitals and clinics, as well as from the iPhone itself, giving millions of Americans direct digital control of their own health information for the first time.

Apple's fellow tech giant has also been in on the march into medical services. In January 2018, Amazon announced a partnership with Berkshire Hathaway and JPMorgan Chase to create a not-for-profit healthcare company for their own employees that promises to employ technology to provide cheaper care than conventional health insurers offer.

Apple's next big contribution is likely to be in making its devices into trusted, secure channels through which medical data can flow. Very much like the app store, third parties will then build useful health services on top. Putting patients' health records on iPhones will make these far more effective. So far, millions of people around the world have already joined medical studies using this infrastructure, participating through iPhones.

All this contributes to Apple's profits by increasing the perceived value of its devices, says Anurag Gupta, a Healthcare Analyst at Gartner, an IT research firm. The firm also hopes that clinicians and insurers will buy and use Apple devices in their work.

Profits might not be an end in themselves but rather a signal from society that the company is succeeding in its mission to provide innovative products that people want. From this perspective, profits are the measure and the reward is the success in delivering to society the more fundamental business purpose.

PROFIT & SOCIETY: UNILEVER

The next category, Profit & Society, describes those businesses that believe in free enterprise but aspire to create businesses with a purpose beyond profit. These are businesses that focus on achieving their economic goals as well as their sustainability goals.

Unilever was born as a solution to a crisis. The company was founded in the 1880s and produced the world's first packaged, branded bar of soap in an effort to stop rampant epidemics and child deaths amidst the grinding poverty and squalor of Victorian England. Nearly 130 years later, there is still a deep sense at Unilever of its social purpose.

Today, Unilever is among the 100 largest companies in the world, generating $58 billion in revenue for 2017 with $6 billion in profit. The company arguably impacts every corner of the world, considering that it has 300 factories around the globe, works with some 76,000 suppliers in 190 countries and produces 400 brands for 2.5 billion customers—an astonishing one in every three people on the planet.

CONNECTING WITH ITS IDENTITY

William Lever, founder of what is now Unilever, had pioneered the Victorian model of paternalistic business. At a time when disease and malnutrition were widespread in Britain, his products were marketed for their health benefits. His employees were decently housed in a purpose-built company town. Lever campaigned for state pensions for the elderly and even provided schooling, healthcare and good wages at palm-oil plantations in the Congo.

It has been reported that Lever routinely slept in the open on top of his mansion; when Paul Polman became Chief Executive of the Anglo-Dutch consumer goods giant, the Dutchman spent a night in Lever's rooftop bed as part of a total immersion in the history of his new firm. It helped persuade him to launch the "Sustainable Living Plan," the name for his attempt to make Unilever the preeminent example of responsible capitalism.

Just before Polman joined from Nestlé, the company had seen revenues fall from €52 billion to €40 billion. The business had lost its focus on consumers and their world. It had become preoccupied with the transition from a conglomerate model to a composite model. According to Polman, Unilever was behind Nestlé and other competitors on the obesity issue and lost market share as a result, and it failed to adapt quickly enough to the growing importance of emerging markets. So not being in tune with society, the incoming CEO realised, had cost the company dearly.

Soon after he took over in 2009, he set out the challenge to double the company's revenue while halving its environmental impact. Like Lever, he insisted that running the firm with close attention to its environmental and social impact was not an act of charity but of self-interest, properly conceived. The Sustainable Living Plan was designed not only to reduce Unilever's environmental footprint and increase its positive social impact but also to double sales and increase long-term profitability.

THE POLMAN DOCTRINE

Polman is a passionate advocate for companies being run sustainably, whether by investing ethically, remunerating staff fairly, or ensuring the actual products are healthy and are produced with the minimum environmental impact. This ethos might not result in quick financial gains, but Polman's view was that by establishing and investing in enduring and sustainable actions, the company would be rewarded alongside society in the longer term.

For example, shortly after Polman became Chief Executive of Unilever in 2009, he said that he only wanted investors who shared his view that Unilever needed to shepherd the Earth's future as carefully as it did its own revenues and profits. Quarterly profit updates were out as Polman believed they encouraged short-term thinking, or as he put it, "Are they really my shareholders if they own my stock for a nanosecond or a few months?"

This initiative led Simon Zadek, a long-time British sustainability campaigner, to state, "This was a new business model."

This stance would obviously have repercussions on shareholders who expected short-term gains from their investment, but Polman was unmoved by their concerns, stating "Unilever has been around for 100-plus years. We want to be around for several hundred more years. So if you buy into this long-term value-creation model, which is equitable, which is shared, which is sustainable, then come and invest with us. If you don't buy into this, I respect you as a human being but don't put your money in our company."

Many companies place shareholder concerns at the heart of their business, but as we have seen, Polman was insistent that this would not be the case for Unilever. His vision went further than the transitory nature of modern business reporting, beyond even focusing on his customer base, by instead considering the whole of society in a similar way to the great industrialists of the past. As a *Fortune* article states, Polman's focus was "not only on how to sell more products for customers, but also on how to sell more products that are good for customers, in a way that benefits suppliers and does not destroy the environment."[78]

Of course, this is not all pure altruism on Polman's behalf. He believes that consumers will increasingly shun those companies that neglect their social responsibilities, which in turn means those that do showcase gender equality, strong employee relations and environmentally responsible practices will be the financial beneficiaries. He does not view employees, suppliers and producers as isolated silos but instead as all part of the wider society. Treating them well not only builds up trust in the brand but also gives them the financial capability to become customers themselves.

78 Vivienne Walt, "Unilever CEO Paul Polman's Plan to Save the World," *Fortune*, February 17 2017, http://fortune.com/2017/02/17/unilever-paul-polman-responsibility-growth/.

Neither, however, is Polman's position just a calculated strategy to boost finances, as on a personal level he has refused increases to his base salary of $1.2 million and on a corporate level he stated, "The real purpose of business has always been to come up with solutions that are relevant to society, to make society better."

While many countries around the world are struggling to create employment and grow their economies, the cost of unsustainable practices is increasing. In 2016, Polman highlighted this issue by pointing out that 9 percent of global GDP is devoted to conflict prevention or wars, while climate change costs an additional 5 percent. He emphasises that if corporations are not clearly showing how they are addressing these themes and wider societal issues, then they will not have a reason to exist.

He said, "There is no business case for enduring poverty and no reason to accept companies that are run for the benefit of a few at a cost to many. For Unilever, shareholder returns are a result of what we do, but not why we are here. For over a hundred years our goal has been to improve the lives of the world's citizens one day and one person at a time."[79] In 2012, the United Nations selected Polman as the only business executive in a group of twenty-six people to craft the seventeen goals that in 2015 became the UN's SDGs, including eliminating poverty and gender inequality. An interview with *Fortune* in early 2017 highlighted how seriously Polman took this responsibility. When asked how much time he dedicates to either Unilever or the lobbying for the SDGs, he stated, "To me it is the same. I don't separate that. I think it is an integral part of the way we run our business."

Finding the right balance between society and business has been at the heart of Polman's strategy at Unilever. However, it is one thing to aspire or claim to be sustainable and another to understand what provides the optimum social value and how to

79 Vivienne Walt, "Unilever CEO Paul Polman's Plan to Save the World," *Fortune*, February 17 2017, http://fortune.com/2017/02/17/unilever-paul-polman-responsibility-growth/.

demonstrate the benefits to all the relevant stakeholders. Reflecting on his own experiences, Polman said, "We are finding out quite rapidly that to be successful long term we have to ask: What do we actually give society to make it better?"

The SDGs were a step toward formalising sustainability expectations for the wider corporate world, but prior to this, Polman had implemented his own plan within his own company—the Unilever Sustainable Living Plan.

THE UNILEVER SUSTAINABLE LIVING PLAN (USLP)

Unilever announced its Sustainable Living Plan in November 2010, presenting its sustainability commitments and targets for the next decade. This plan would redefine the company's purpose and vision and Polman saw it as not only central to the company's core business strategy but as a revolution, or in his own words, a "new business model."

When some companies grow in scale, they take the calculated stance that increased production and demands on resources mean that there will be a necessary amount of social or environmental collateral. Polman was clear that at Unilever, he expected the reverse to be the case: the plan aims to double the size of the business while lowering its environmental impact, including a 50 percent reduction in its ecological footprint by 2020.

These were not just vague pledges either, as the company set itself a series of targets up until 2020, applying to every Unilever product and brand, while covering social, economic and environmental factors. The company listed specific targets for fifty metrics, including total water consumption and emissions of greenhouse gas, but there were three headline objectives:

1. To help more than 1 billion people take action to improve their health and well-being

2. To halve the environmental footprint of the making and use of its products (including sourcing 100 percent of its agricultural raw materials sustainably)
3. To enhance the livelihoods of hundreds of thousands of people in its supply chain (such as by linking more than half a million smallholder farmers and small-scale distributors to its supply chain)

When the Sustainable Living Plan was originally announced, Jonathon Porritt, Founder and Director of Forum for the Future, described it as "the best plan out there for big global companies," with the caveat that "success can only be judged in terms of what is delivered." With the plan now in its ninth year, we can begin to review and analyse its impact.

Sue Garrard, Senior Vice President of Sustainable Business Development and Communications at Unilever, made it clear that "what we had to do was to really stretch ourselves and while we might fail, what we would achieve is to change the mindset of the whole way of thinking in the business." As we will see, that change in mindset has taken place, transcending beyond Unilever.[80]

USLP Successes

Some of the results of the plan are simple to measure and tell a clear story. Between Polman's joining in early 2009 and August 2017, there were significant reductions in a series of important business processes, including emissions (–43 percent), water usage (–38 percent) and waste (–96 percent) per unit of production. At the same time, investment (including capital spending, research, branding and marketing) rose from 18 to 20 percent of sales and tax payments increased from 25 to 30 percent of underlying profits.

80 Globescan Webinar 2017. Sue Garrand. *Sustainability Leaders Survey*. https://globescan.com/webinar-recap-the-2017-sustainability-leaders-survey/

In addition, *The Economist* suggests that the plan may also have boosted Unilever's share price, pointing out that in the five years after unveiling the plan, shares rose by more than 40 percent. This is even more impressive when we consider the wider economic environment the company was operating in, as Unilever's main rival, Procter & Gamble of America, was in its own crisis because reduced profit forecasts resulted in the loss of its CEO. AllianceBernstein had more good news for Unilever shareholders when it revealed the corporation's global market share had risen from 16 to 18 percent between 2008 and 2017.

Critics might argue that the company has not yet hit its target to double its revenue from €40 billion to €80 billion and in fact, by early 2017, it had only achieved a tenth of this growth. However, this €4 billion growth was heavily affected by large currency fluctuations, and it translated to a more impressive €10 billion while also fostering a "growth mentality" within the company that sets it up well for future progress.

Factors like engagement are less tangible and thus more difficult to measure, but Polman believes there is strong evidence that the plan has had benefits across employees, customers and other stakeholders. Polman gives the example of employees' engagement scores being "way off the charts" compared to their peers, despite having had a three-year pay freeze, which he believes shows that they support Unilever's strategy.

Another positive indication that Unilever's approach has been well received is that its Sustainable Living brands are growing more than 50 percent faster than other departments and accounted for 60 percent of growth in 2016. In addition, research conducted by the company to understand the drivers of consumer purchasing habits found that over half already buy or want to buy sustainably.

Responding to these positive signs, Polman was keen to highlight the impact the plan has had, stating, "There is no doubt that the Unilever Sustainable Living Plan is making us more competitive by helping us to build our brands and spur innovation, strengthen our supply chain, reduce our risks, lower our costs and build trust in our business. It is helping Unilever to serve society and our many consumers and in doing so, create value for shareholders."

Polman's message seems to be getting heard by consumers. In GlobeScan's 2017 survey on Sustainability Leaders, one question asked respondents what specific companies they think are leaders in integrating sustainability into their business strategy. Unilever achieved a 45 percent share of voice, almost double that of Patagonia, which came in second with 23 percent. A similar question focused on climate change and Unilever again topped the responses with 28 percent, with Ikea the closest consumer-goods challenger at 11 percent.[81]

However, Unilever is keen to point out that in order to be an integral part of their business strategy, sustainability success has to be carefully measured, or as Polman says, "We drive this using hard numbers, not fluffy feelings and hunches." One aspect of this is how the company is leading the way on "integrated reporting," the movement to incorporate societal profit and loss statements into annual reports. The company is also careful not to sugarcoat the outcomes in these reports, highlighting the areas that need significant improvements alongside the successes that many companies would prefer to focus on.

Reflecting on the changes he has seen since joining, Polman remarked, "When I came here, this company had done everything you can think of. Created sustainable initiatives, sustainable fishery, sustainable agriculture round tables, but we were only 10 percent sustainable. Now we're 65 percent sustainable." Looking further afield, he is encouraged by the influence Unilever has had

81 The GlobeScan Sustainability Leaders. "The GlobeScan Sustainability Survey". *GlobeScan*. December 7 2017. https://globescan.com/wp-content/uploads/2017/07/GSS-Leaders-2017-Survey-Report.pdf

on the wider corporate world's attitude to sustainability, observing, "Now you have companies like Ikea or Apple or Facebook buying green energy. You have companies like Dow and Solvay or Schneider being very active in Paris on the climate negotiations."

USLP CHALLENGES

Despite the successes, there have been suggestions that the initial positivity around this approach is beginning to fade and that traditional business interests are beginning to reassert themselves. While Unilever share values may be well above where they were prior to the plan, they fell 2 percent in 2017, while the S&P 500 increased 25 percent. As we have seen, Polman has already shown a certain ambivalence toward shareholders, which can be tolerated when finances are good, but along with the self-imposed restrictions and tough targets, it can put him at risk when the weather changes for the worse.

While Unilever claims that 80 percent of its investors see its sustainable approach as boosting long-term value, Jefferies analyst Martin Deboo told *Forbes*, "A minority of investors I speak to give two hoots about Unilever's Sustainable Living Plan." Deboo suggests that good intentions are beginning to give way to business realities now that the novelty has worn off, saying that "people indulged Unilever on USLP in the early years when the reporting numbers were going well. Now they want to hear more muscular language about earnings and returns."

Deboo believes that Unilever is becoming more of a niche investment for those who share similar concerns, but it isn't that attractive to traditional investors. Linda Scott of Oxford University's Saïd Business School acknowledges that Unilever is pushing this agenda further than other companies but is concerned about the practicalities of refocusing 400 brands "on the good the product can do." She believes that the scale of this change requires time and this is a potential cause of friction for impatient shareholders.

Switching focus to conditions inside Unilever, there are also concerns around remuneration. Polman presented employee positivity toward the brand, despite a lack of pay raises, as a sign they bought into the ethos. That goodwill may not last, however, as pay as a share of the firm's output has fallen from 46 percent to 39 percent. On the other hand, this approach has enabled Unilever to maintain steady staff numbers when others have been forced to make cuts.

To understand how Unilever's policies were translating to its employees around the globe, Oxfam investigated working conditions in a Vietnam factory the company had been using since 1995. Oxfam found that Unilever's stated principles were routinely ignored, including language regarding fair pay. Rachel Wilshaw of Oxfam explained, "The company didn't understand that though they were paying above the minimum legal wage, it was far below a living wage."

This incident may have been an honest mistake due to a lack of familiarity with local practices, but exacerbating the issue is that those near the top have received an average 24 percent more remuneration. Things appear worse still when looking at Polman's most recent remuneration. Despite previously claiming he is embarrassed by his wage and that he would happily work for free,[82] he received a 39 percent increase in pay in 2018,[83] leading to numerous suggestions that there could be a shareholder revolt.

Another issue for Unilever is that Unilever's Sustainable Living Plan has not met all its targets. In mid-2016, the company admitted it would fail to meet its goals of halving its products'

---

82 Scheherazade Daneshkhu, "Unilever Chief Executive's Pay Cut by 20% in 2016," *Financial Times*, February 28, 2017, https://www.ft.com/content/e7293e0e-fddf-11e6-8d8e-a5e3738f9ae4.

83 Scheherazade Daneshkhu, "Unilever Chief Paul Polman's Pay Rises 40 Percent," *Financial Times*, February 28, 2018, https://www.ft.com/content/5559a39c-1cb0-11e8-aaca-4574d7dabfb6.

environmental impact by 2020, instead switching the target date to 2030. One reason for this is that its growth markets coincide with some of the most difficult regions for implementing the sustainability goals. While the company has 76,000 suppliers and operates in 190 countries, almost 60 percent of its turnover is now from emerging markets, many of which have looser regulations on environmental issues as they strive to grow enough to rival the traditional leaders.

This highlights the wider challenge facing Unilever; if it hopes to meet its USLP targets, then it's going to have to change consumer behaviour, globally. Early in the plan's life, the company discovered that across its product range, an average of 68 percent of greenhouse gas emissions in the life cycle occurred only after consumers purchased the product. In the 2016 report, Unilever admitted that the greenhouse gases associated with its products had increased 6 percent, rather than decreasing by 50 percent, indicating that it was still battling with educating or persuading its user base regarding best sustainability practices.

Despite these issues, there is a widespread acknowledgment that Unilever is genuine in its intentions. After the Oxfam Vietnam report, Unilever took action to remedy the problem, reviewing global factory worker wages, while also introducing tougher requirements for suppliers. Rachel Wilshaw, Ethical Trade Manager at nonprofit Oxfam, responded to this with praise for Polman: "Here was a company where, because of the leadership, it was open to the problems we threw at them." However, she also gave a reminder of the realities of commerce faced by the company: "At the end of the day Unilever is a shareholder-owned business and shareholders are voracious for profits."[84]

There are echoes here of William Lever's earlier experiences, when shareholder pressure in the 1920s forced him to scale back

84 Vivienne Walt, "Unilever CEO Paul Polman's Plan to Save the World," *Fortune*, February 2017, http://fortune.com/2017/02/17/unilever-paul-polman-responsibility-growth/.

his own ambitions. Polman may have moved to reduce the short-termism of quarterly results, but with the share price in decline, his remaining time with Unilever is likely to be a difficult balancing act on this front.

HOSTILE TAKEOVER

Even with the challenges it faces, Unilever has found its strong social contract serves it well in times of crisis. In early 2017, Unilever received a surprise takeover bid from Kraft Heinz, backed by Warren Buffett and 3G Capital, a fund with a reputation for cost-cutting. With the potential to be the second largest corporate deal in history, the valuation may have been the key issue for many in Polman's position. However, he saw Kraft's social contract to be completely at odds with the one he had initiated at Unilever, describing the bid as "clearly a clash between a long-term, sustainable business model for multiple stakeholders and a model that is entirely focused on shareholder primacy," or even more bluntly, "a clash between people who think about billions of people in the world and some people that think about a few billionaires."

The Economist described Kraft as a "roll-up," explaining it "relies on acquisitions and cost cuts to mask low growth. Its sales have declined for the past nine quarters. Roll-up strategies usually end badly for investors. Still, cheap debt means that, while such firms remain on a winning streak, they can operate on a vastly greater scale than before." There were black marks against the deal for someone who had always promoted an alternative to this aggressive shareholder primacy business model.

The Unilever response was rapid. News broke of the proposal on Friday and it was basically dead by Sunday. The fierce rejection was largely based on this mismatch in corporate culture, though it was also expected that Unilever shareholders would not be receptive to a debt-led bid that would have meant it was basically funded by their own money. By being decisive, Unilever was able to avoid letting the approach turn into a hostile takeover and an uncertain future. Garrard summarised Unilever's position as follows: "we had the belief that we were fighting for a way of doing business that makes a difference."[85]

Key to this swift and firm rejection was the confidence that the majority of stakeholders had bought into Unilever's social contract. "We have a board that is very supportive and understands our business model," said Polman. Seventy percent of shareholders had held shares for seven or more years, so they were more focused on the longer-term vision than short-term gains. Polman was even able to mobilise those within his network to persuade Buffett against continuing with the bid. "Warren was approached by probably more people than he expected," Polman revealed.

If Polman had not ingrained the social contract so deeply within all aspects of the business, then any one group could have caused significant problems without the rejection of such a deal. The long-term, socially conscious view won out on this occasion, because everyone bought into the Unilever philosophy.

IS THIS THE NEW MODEL OF CAPITALISM?

The comprehensive rejection of the Kraft Heinz bid shows how big the gap still is between Unilever's approach and that of many of its corporate peers. Polman is not expected to remain as CEO for much longer, but in his remaining time at the company, he is keen to persuade others to follow this lead.

Polman sees the responsibilities of business differently from most in his position, going so far as to tell the London School of Economics, "I always say I represent one of the biggest NGOs." As the *Financial Times* said, with pre-tax profits over €7 billion,

85 Globescan Webinar 2017. Sue Garrand. *Sustainability Leaders Survey*. https://globescan.com/webinar-recap-the-2017-sustainability-leaders-survey/

Unilever "is not most people's idea of an NGO."[86] However, the publication goes on to concede that Polman's approach is an exciting new way to conduct business as he "attempts to balance long-term profitability with a mantra of increasing sustainability."

This dedication to the environment and sustainable practices led to praise from actual NGOs, though even they were sceptical that this approach could work in the business world. The World Wildlife Fund's Director General put it this way: "Everybody was just wondering: is he crazy? Is he going to be sacked six months later?" The fact that during his tenure Unilever's total shareholder return was ahead of his old company Nestlé and significantly more than P&G, meant that he not only survived but became a recognised leader in this new way of commercial thinking.

There are still enough naysayers to cast some doubt on the effectiveness of his strategy and the legacy it will leave. There have already been cases of business practicalities overriding sustainable planning, such as when a smaller deodorant failed to win consumers away from the larger packaged rivals.

Polman himself worries that those driving the investments in business are not taking on enough responsibility, which in turn puts the pressure on his approach rather than those actively causing harm. When speaking to portfolio managers in 2018, Polman implied that they had to take a more mature and holistic view of their jobs, telling them to put the spotlight on those that did not have socially responsible strategies, rather than continually asking why companies like Unilever do integrate environmental, social and governance concerns. He further emphasised this point by challenging them as to why he had not received a single question about climate change, diversity, or human rights in over a decade of earnings calls.

Despite the revised targets and setbacks to the original plan,

---

86 M.Skapinker and S.Daneshkhu, "Can Unilever's Paul Polman Change the Way We Do Business?" *Financial Times*, September 29, 2016. https://www.ft.com/content/e6696b4a-8505-11e6-8897-2359a58ac7a5

Polman remains convinced his ideas will leave the wider business landscape in better shape. He sees the potential in the next generation, pointing out that the company's values are so popular with millennials that they receive 1.8 million applications a year.

We will let Polman have the last word on the matter: "If business cannot show what positive impact it has, why should the citizens of the world let business be around?"

SOCIETY FIRST: PATAGONIA

Society First companies are for-profit corporate entities that commit to making a positive impact on society, workers, the community and the environment—in addition to profit—in their legally defined goals. While they are not immune to the financial necessities of the business world, they prioritise their social contract above all else. Based on my research, a company that I believe exemplifies the Society First type is the outdoor clothing manufacturer Patagonia.

Patagonia provides a compelling example for this new type of company as it does not operate in pursuit of continual annual profit growth. Instead, Patagonia's core principles include producing sustainably made clothing that creates as little waste as possible in the process and selling products that are made to last as long as possible, so consumers do not need to purchase new products each year.[87] This business model may seem radical for a company operating in the fashion industry, in which ever-changing trends drive new sales each season, but it is also a clever way of demonstrating the confidence it has in the quality and durability of its product.

When founder Yvon Chouinard figured out the company's

---

87 Alec Banks. "5 Things Patagonia Teaches us About Branding for the Long Haul." *The Hundreds*. October 6, 2016. https://thehundreds.com/blogs/content/5-things-patagonia-teaches-us-about-branding-for-the-long-haul.

costs, profits and growth rate, he did a radical thing: he put a cap on the growth of the business. For him, the impact of the company on society was more important than profits.[88]

This is not to say that profits have not been forthcoming. Between 2009 and 2013, Patagonia doubled its revenue to more than $500 million and by 2016, it had surpassed $800 million while employing more than 2,000 employees. While these are impressive figures, they can be contextualised by comparing them with competitors such as The North Face and Columbia, which recorded $2 billion and $2.3 billion in sales respectively. While Patagonia may be smaller, it is growing faster and its positioning has given it a shield against the commercial volatility that has seen many other brands fall out of fashion.[89]

As we will discover, Patagonia's steady rise should not be seen as being hindered or constrained by sticking to its core principles; actually, in many ways, its success is based on those very values.

LET MY PEOPLE GO SURFING

In this new model of societal engagement, Patagonia must account for all stakeholders in its approach. Employees, customers and the environment all have a say. Societal engagement is truly baked into the identity of this company.

In one of its first attempts at engaging with stakeholders, Patagonia's 1985 "1 Percent for the Planet" campaign effectively donated 1 percent of all sales to grassroots environmental groups. When questioned about the donations, founder Chouinard responded, "You have to get away from the idea that it's philanthropy. I look at it as a cost of doing business. Every business should say, "We're

88 Louise Keefe, Ron Milam, and Laura Woodwar. "Patagonia Case Assignment." *MSOD 617*. September 23, 2013.

89 Alec Banks. "5 Things Patagonia Teaches us About Branding for the Long Haul." *The Hundreds*. October 6, 2016. https://thehundreds.com/blogs/content/5-things-patagonia-teaches-us-about-branding-for-the-long-haul.

polluters, we're using our nonrenewable resources and therefore we should tax ourselves. Being part of [1 percent for the Planet] is also good for business...Think of it as a marketing cost."[90] In 2015, the company revealed that since 1985, it had donated more than $70 million in cash and services as part of this "Earth Tax."[91]

The company continues to refine and expand its mission; in September of 2013, it launched a campaign called "The Responsible Economy," a form of capitalism based on necessity rather than wants. This was a radical break from standard corporate convention, as it set out to limit the company's own growth by calling on consumers and businesses alike to rethink disposability and consider an economy that is not based on consumption. Patagonia argued that global social issues such as climate change, toxic pollution and resource depletion were just symptoms of a larger problem that drives this "consumption mentality."[92]

This approach is reflected in Patagonia's mission statement: "Build the best product, cause no unnecessary harm, use business to inspire and implement solutions to the environmental crisis."[93]

Patagonia's values are largely a reflection of their founder's. The company grew organically out of Chouinard's passion for climbing and the outdoors, as they state, "Our values reflect those of a business started by a band of climbers and surfers and the minimalist style they promoted. For us at Patagonia, a love of wild and beautiful places demands participation in the fight to save them."[94]

---

90 D.O'Rourke and R.Strand, "Patagonia: Driving Sustainable Innovation by Embracing Tensions," *Harvard Business Review*. February 16 2016. https://hbr.org/product/patagonia-driving-sustainable-innovation-by-embracing-tensions/B5853-PDF-ENG

91 Patagonia. "Our Earth Tax- Patagonia Environmental + Social Initiatives 2015." *Patagonia*. September 9, 2015. https://www.patagonia.com/blog/2015/09/our-earth-tax-patagonia-environmental-social-initiatives-2015/

92 Jonathan James Carter. "Patagonia: Transmitting Sustainability." *European University Business School*. January 26, 2015.

93 Patagonia. "Patagonia's Mission Statement." *Patagonia*. https://www.patagonia.com/company-info.html

94 Patagonia. "Patagonia's Mission Statement." *Patagonia*. https://www.patagonia.com/company-info.html

Chouinard himself is an unlikely business leader, claiming he "never even wanted to be in business. But I hang onto Patagonia because it's my resource to do something good. It's a way to demonstrate that corporations can lead examined lives." This passion for showing there is an alternative way that businesses can conduct themselves led him to write a book in 2005, called *Let My People Go Surfing: The Education of a Reluctant Businessman.*[95] Following its publication, Chouinard explained that the original concept for the book was for it just to be a "philosophical manual for the employees of Patagonia," but its success outgrew these intentions. His mantra for the company was as follows: "Lead an examined life; Clean up our own life; Do our penance; Support civil democracy; and Influence other companies" connected with an increasingly environmentally conscious public.[96]

Often when a company is forced into change, media-friendly soundbites about social issues will be treated with suspicion, dismissed as mere marketing jargon intended to deflect attention from the ongoing problems. However, there are few today who view Patagonia's approach as anything other than 100 percent authentic, placing philanthropy and environmentalism at the heart of the business. Chouinard challenged the general perception that to become a philanthropist you first have to have been a profit-focused capitalist, stating, "Most people want to do good things, but don't. At Patagonia, it's an essential part of your life."[97]

Whether inspired by Patagonia or the transparency of social media in the New Normal, an increasing number of companies are beginning to draw more attention to their own brands and

---

95 Yvon Chouinard, *Let My People Go Surfing: The Education of a Reluctant Businessman* (New York: Penguin, 2005).

96 Alabama Chanin. "Patagonia: An Examined Life." *AlabamaChanin Journal.* August 5, 2013. http://journal.alabamachanin.com/2013/08/patagonia-an-examined-life/.

97 Bloomberg. "A Passion for the Planet". *Bloomberg Businessweek.* August 21, 2006. https://www.bloomberg.com/news/articles/2006-08-20/a-passion-for-the-planet

values, while CEOs have been much more vocal on a number of social issues, such as discrimination, gender pay, climate change and gun ownership.

Chouinard will undoubtedly be encouraged to see the social initiatives at companies like TOMS Shoes, Levi Strauss, Warby Parker and Smile Squared, but as TOMS also discovered, there are always obstacles to overcome in order to stay true to a socially beneficial strategy.[98]

TROUBLED WATERS

In Patagonia's early days, demand for its products constantly exceeded supply, which meant internally there was a somewhat cursory attitude toward the company's financial affairs and strategic planning.

Despite this success, Chouinard and Patagonia were to reach a vital crossroads that would challenge the company's commitment to sustainability and ultimately lead it to fully embracing a radical new approach to business. It came in the early '90s, when the company's rapid growth left it stretched too thin. Credit was cut off, which meant inventory had to be dumped below its cost in order to meet the debts. The painful outcome for Chouinard was the company losing 20 percent of its workforce.

At this time, Chouinard was advised to sell his company, which was a tempting idea, as alongside his ingrained disdain for the business world, he would be able to devote the bulk of the $100 million price to environmentally beneficial campaigns. Chouinard said he "seriously considered it," but instead of quitting, he refocused his agenda. He had "made the same mistakes every other company makes. I decided the best thing I could do was

98 Mike Montgomery, "What Entrepreneurs Can Learn from the Philanthropic Struggles of TOMS Shoes," *Forbes*, April 28, 2015. https://www.forbes.com/sites/mikemontgomery/2015/04/28/how-entrepreneurs-can-avoid-the-philanthropy-pitfalls/

to get profitable again, live a more examined corporate life and influence other companies to do the same."[99]

Other companies have experienced their own difficulties in the pursuit of an authentic social contract. The aforementioned TOMS had an apparently laudable initiative to donate a pair of shoes to children living in poverty for every pair they sold, but it was criticised for not dealing with, or fixing, the core issues that had led to the community experiencing economic difficulties.[100] More recently, Mastercard faced a significant backlash when it launched a campaign to generate attention around the 2018 World Cup, in which it stated it would donate 10,000 meals to hungry children for every goal scored by two prominent players. Critics claimed that an issue as important as child starvation should not be left to chance and if a company could afford to meet this obligation, then it should just do it without conditions.[101]

These incidents show the troubles that even examples of a Society First company can experience when just dipping a toe into the supposedly reputationally beneficial world of sustainability, highlighting the importance of authenticity and having a leader who can see the bigger picture and how it links with every part of the strategy. As Patagonia has been a sustainability trailblazer, it has faced a number of hurdles along its journey, but it hopes that by overcoming these issues, it can inspire others to follow.

RIDING THE WAVE

In response to Patagonia's problems, the company reviewed its

99 Louise Keefe, Ron Milam, and Laura Woodwar. "Patagonia Case Assignment." *MSOD 617*. September 23, 2013.

100 Mike Montgomery. "What Entrepreneurs can Learn from the Philanthropic Struggles of TOM Shoes." *Forbes*. April 28, 2015. https://www.forbes.com/sites/mikemontgomery/2015/04/28/how-entrepreneurs-can-avoid-the-philanthropy-pitfalls/#2de33ae91c38

101 John Harrington. "Mastercard Drops 'Goals for Meals' Campaign after Backlash." *PR Week*. June 5, 2018. https://www.prweek.com/article/1466558/mastercard-drops-goals-for-meals-campaign-backlash

finances and production strategy, while vowing to become debt-free, which it has since achieved. However, it took no shortcuts on the way to reaching this goal, as evidenced by the decision in 1996 to invest in the more environmentally friendly organic cotton and other sustainable materials, though the move initially tripled supply costs.

Even more surprisingly, rather than being tempted to use these new materials, which included recycled drink bottles, as an excuse to supply lower-quality goods, the company took the exact opposite approach and committed to increasing the durability of its products. This was a bold move in a society so used to fashions changing with the seasons and in which the concept of "planned obsolescence" means that many are happy to upgrade their phone handsets every year.

With so many positive social initiatives, it would be easy for the company to just put all the focus on its successes and bask in the resulting applause. However, Chouinard holds himself and the company to higher standards and insists on publicly listing out the environmental damage caused by its actions. In addition, the company has a "Worn Wear" programme that aims to keep used Patagonia products out of landfills by facilitating a trade-in option via its own exchange site, repairing products or recycling them if the damage is too great.[102]

If a company is actively campaigning for its customers to reuse and recycle rather than buying again, does this not put its whole model at risk? In fact, Patagonia's new approach found a receptive audience that appreciated the socially responsible message. This helped build trust in the company's motivations, resulting in a loyalty that went beyond the quality of the product itself. Patagonia's experiences show that by incorporating strong values

---

102 Alec Banks. "5 Things Patagonia Teaches us About Branding for the Long Haul." *The Hundreds*. October 6, 2016. https://thehundreds.com/blogs/content/5-things-patagonia-teaches-us-about-branding-for-the-long-haul.

and an ethical focus within their leadership, companies can strive while acting as role models for those with an authentic desire to make a positive difference.

Patagonia's vision is not limited to external concerns such as its "Earth Tax" or donating more than $70 million in products and services to environmental causes and organisations since 1986. One of its key operating principles is employee centricity. This manifests itself in initiatives like flexible working hours (perhaps when the waves are enticing at nearby surfing locations), job sharing, equal parental leave for both mothers and fathers, on-site childcare, paying for a nanny or partner to accompany parents who need to travel for work, and the option to take fully paid two-month sabbaticals to work on environmental projects.[103]

This has led to employees becoming strong advocates for the Patagonia brand, demonstrated by 100 percent of women returning to the company after maternity leave in the five years between 2012 and 2016. This compares favourably to the US average of 79 percent and enables the company to maintain a perfect gender balance of 50 percent females in both management and senior leadership positions. In addition, the next generation of employees is often found among the children who have been through the on-site childcare system and the company claims that they are its best product. President Obama recognised Patagonia's family-centric achievements in 2015, acknowledging CEO Rose Marcario as a "Champion of Change for Working Families."[104]

When people work for Patagonia, or for any authentic business, they know what they are signing up for. People come to the company because they want to be there. The shared goals and ethos minimise disputes. There might be passionate dis-

---

103 Seth Stevenson. "Patagonia's Founder is America's Most Unlikely Business Guru." *The Wall Street Journal.* April 26, 2012. https://www.wsj.com/articles/SB10001424052702303513404577352221465986612

104 Alec Banks. "5 Things Patagonia Teaches us About Branding for the Long Haul." *The Hundreds.* October 6, 2016. https://thehundreds.com/blogs/content/5-things-patagonia-teaches-us-about-branding-for-the-long-haul.

agreements, but that's because they care about the mission of the business, not because they disagree on the direction. Their direction has already been set.

SUSTAINABILITY ALL THE WAY

Entwined in Patagonia's identity is its commitment to environmental and social causes. In the mid-'90s, the company was part of President Clinton's Apparel Industry Partnership, a task force that led it to become a founding member of the Fair Labor Association. Its branding and marketing strategy has never been complicated or difficult to articulate, because its values are 100 percent consistent with the firm's behaviour. Consumers living in today's split society appreciate this; they feel like their wants and needs are listened to.[105]

As previously discussed, in order to make good on its mission, Patagonia revamped its entire supply chain, switching to organic cotton and recycled materials in the 1990s and then other unusual sources, such as hemp and recycled polyester from plastic drink bottles. This was a calculated risk due to procurement constraints and increased material costs that other companies were wary of because of the perceived high costs and decentralised farming.

Patagonia believed the risk was outweighed by the company's internal ethos. In the end, even companies on the scale of Walmart sought Patagonia's advice on how best to source organic cotton. This inquiry flourished into a partnership, out of which grew the Sustainable Apparel Coalition in 2010, which seeks to develop a more sustainable apparel industry. Brands like Nike, Adidas, Levi Strauss and Gap were invited join and as of 2018,

105 Patagonia. "Patagonia and Social Responsibility in the Supply Chain: A History." *Patagonia.* January 2018. https://www.patagonia.com/corporate-responsibility-history.html

there are more than 100 coalition members, accounting for over a third of all clothing and footwear produced globally.[106]

These companies didn't just say the right thing; they did it, too. Levi Strauss, for example, spent eighteen months redesigning its processes in order to save 45 million gallons of water and the energy needed to heat it. As with Patagonia, it discovered this benefitted not just society but also the company's balance sheet. As Michael Kobori, Levi's VP of Social and Environmental Sustainability, explained, "The business savings costs are real." Phil Graves, Patagonia's Director of Corporate Development, echoed Kobori's sentiments about how this long-term approach can be most effective, stating, "It does come down to cost. A lot of companies want to do the right thing but are afraid of a negative hit on next quarter's earnings. When we switched to organic cotton in 1996, it initially hurt our bottom line, but it was a great decision looking back. Other companies might not be willing to take the long view."[107]

Chouinard considered every step of the company's supply chain and worked to move the whole thing in a sustainable direction with each step. The brand commissioned an environmental impact assessment to measure the amounts of water, energy and chemicals that were used to make Patagonia clothing, a study that identified its material supply chains as the "most significant contributors to Patagonia's environmental footprint."

Director of Materials Innovation and Development Matt Dwyer described it this way: "We are explicitly trying to build the absolute best product in terms of durability, functionality, fit, multi-functionality, as well as the design attributes such as being long-lasting, timeless, durable and doing exactly what we say it

106 Seth Stevenson. "Patagonia's Founder is America's Most Unlikely Business Guru." *The Wall Street Journal.* April 26, 2012. https://www.wsj.com/articles/SB10001424052702303513404577352221465986612

107 Dara O'Rourke and Robert Strand, "Patagonia: Driving Sustainable Innovation by Embracing Tensions," *Harvard Business Review* (2016).

will. This is hands down the number one goal. We continuously look for ways to minimise environmental harm while building the best product."[108]

Patagonia's basic strategy is to build a quality product while being responsible and choosing to invest in a supply chain that looks for raw material sources close to the factory the company is manufacturing in. They source from long-term partners with operations in multiple countries and cap each factory at 25 percent capacity to ensure that if the company should leave, the impact on the community wouldn't be devastating.[109]

"We like to know how the people in the supply chain are being managed," says COO Doug Freeman. "We care deeply about our environmental footprint and we want to build the best product that will be used by people for a very long time—we are against fast fashion and landfills, which lead to our CO_2 problem. We are very proud that some of our most popular styles such as our Snap-T fleece and baggies are styles we introduced twenty to thirty years ago." Part of what makes the company's supply chain manageable is that it is kept relatively small, with only 190 suppliers total.[110]

Rick Ridgeway, Vice President of Public Engagement, explains how sustainability is crucial to the company: "Central to the evolution of my own position at Patagonia is the strategy of decentralising and integrating sustainability within the organisation. That's a big deal. It's the natural evolution of any company's commitment to sustainability that's genuine. If a company's really

108 "HeiQ and Patagonia Announce Their Exclusive Strategic Research Partnership to Explore Novel Ways for Sustainable Water Repellence," *HEIQ*. February 6 2017. https://heiq.com/2017/02/06/heiq-and-patagonia-announce-their-exclusive-strategic-research-partnership-to-explore-novel-ways-for-sustainable-water-repellence/

109 Patagonia. "Patagonia's Factory List." *Patagonia*. July 8, 2008. https://www.patagonia.com/blog/2008/07/patagonias-fact/

110 Louise Keefe, Ron Milam, and Laura Woodwar. "Patagonia Case Assignment." *MSOD 617*. September 23, 2013.

going to embrace sustainability issues, then it has to figure out how to integrate it into the warp and weft of the organisation."[111]

In a daring and admirable marketing move, the company showcased this commitment by taking out a full-page advertisement in *The New York Times* with a boldface headline: "Don't Buy This Jacket." Below the words was a picture of the fleece jacket in question and the ad copy listed how much water was wasted and carbon emitted in the course of its construction. This was partially in response to research Patagonia had conducted, which concluded that the single most valuable sustainable contribution that its customers can make is to keep using their garments for as long as possible, minimising CO_2 emissions, waste output and water usage associated with the production of replacements.

In response to the advert, Harvard Business School Professor Forest Reinhardt said, "I've never seen a company tell customers to buy less of its product. It's a fascinating initiative."[112] Patagonia's sales actually increased by a third that year, though Chouinard insists this was through attracting new customers from competitors, rather than a wider increase in consumption and therefore potential waste. By refusing to condescend to or exploit its customers, the company had managed to create a passionate group of brand evangelists who could spread the word in place of further paid advertisements.

This campaign was consistent with Patagonia's Common Threads Initiative, the call to reduce new purchases, resell, repair where possible and recycle when necessary. These were not just empty words, as Patagonia operates North America's largest apparel repair facility, responsible for more than 40,000 repairs each year and has also published over forty repair guides on its

111 Dara O'Rourke and Robert Strand, "Patagonia: Driving Sustainable Innovation by Embracing Tensions," *Harvard Business Review.* (2016).

112 R.Casadesus-Masanell, K.Hyunjin and F.Reinhardt, "Patagonia," *Harvard Business School Case* 711-020, August 2010 (revised October 2010).

website. In addition, the company runs its own reselling system and encourages people to send in all of their products that need to be recycled, so it can reuse the fibres rather than letting them end up in a landfill. In turn, the clothes made from recycled materials were produced with the inherent intent that they themselves could also be recycled.

Patagonia's ambitions for change go beyond the clothing industry and in 2014, the company established an internal venture capital fund called "$20 Million & Change." This fund was designed to aid responsible start-up companies that could grow with similar principles ingrained within their strategies from an early stage. Phil Graves, who also led this initiative, revealed the ideal criteria for this investment: "We only invest in partners that are 100 percent aligned on mission and values. We also have a sweet spot where the company is not only like-minded, but also small enough that our investment would provide meaningful capital to them."[113]

Not every initiative has worked for Patagonia, but by authentically attempting to improve what a corporate social contract can be, the company shows the way for others. As COO Doug Freeman says, "We have a toolbox and we opened it up to the industry, but it's naïve to think we have everything figured out." Following Patagonia's lead, other companies, like TOMS and Mastercard, refused to be put off by the negative response to their social initiatives and instead opted to commit to the sentiment behind the execution and revise their offerings. TOMS now donates birth kits, gives money for clean water and sources its donated shoes from local producers. Mastercard adjusted its campaign to eliminate luck and instead committed to supplying one million meals in 2018,[114] in addition to the 400,000 it had

113 Louise Keefe, Ron Milam, and Laura Woodwar. "Patagonia Case Assignment." *MSOD 617*. September 23, 2013.

114 Mike Montgomery. "What Entrepreneurs can Learn from the Philanthropic Struggles of TOM Shoes." *Forbes*. April 28, 2015. https://www.forbes.com/sites/mikemontgomery/2015/04/28/how-entrepreneurs-can-avoid-the-philanthropy-pitfalls/#2de33ae91c38

already supplied as part of the campaign. Chouinard has always wanted to inspire other businesses to minimise their impact on the environment and these sorts of initiatives are proof that his message is spreading and bearing fruit.

GOING THE B MILE

In 2012, Patagonia registered as a Benefit corporation, a type of for-profit corporate entity that places an emphasis on long-term mission alignment and value creation. Traditional companies are constrained by a responsibility to ultimately maximise financial returns for shareholders. This means that before being greenlit, every socially responsible initiative first has to be justified in terms of creating shareholder value.

This view is anathema to a company like Patagonia, which considers sustainability and social responsibility to be at the core of its ethos. B Corps provide an attractive alternative, as they are required to go beyond maximising share value by creating public benefit. This is defined as a material positive impact on society and the environment, i.e., maximum positive externalities and minimum negative.[115]

A benefit corporation's directors and officers operate the business with the same authority as a traditional corporation but are required to consider the impact of their decisions not only on shareholders but also on society and the environment. In a traditional corporation, shareholders judge the company's financial performance; with a benefit corporation, shareholders judge performance based on the company's social, environmental and financial performance.

Transparency provisions also require B Corps to publish annual benefit reports assessing their social and environmental

115 Seth Stevenson. "Patagonia's Founder is America's Most Unlikely Business Guru." *The Wall Street Journal.* April 26, 2012. https://www.wsj.com/articles/SB10001424052702303513404577352221465986612

performance using a comprehensive, credible, independent and transparent third-party standard.

Typical major provisions of a benefit corporation are:

Purpose

- It shall create general public benefit.
- It shall have the right to name specific public benefit purposes (e.g., 50 percent of profits to charity).
- The creation of public benefit is in the best interests of the benefit corporation.

Accountability

- Directors' duties are to make decisions in the best interests of the corporation.
- Directors and officers shall consider the effect of decisions on shareholders, employees, suppliers, customers, the community and the environment (together, the "stakeholders").

Transparency

- The corporation shall publish an annual Benefit Report in accordance with recognised third-party standards for defining, reporting and assessing social and environmental performance.
- The Benefit Report is 1) delivered to all shareholders and 2) published on a public website, with the exclusion of proprietary data.

This new corporate philosophy is much closer to the Patagonia mindset, so it was no surprise that the company became the first California company to register as a benefit corporation, just days after the state legislation was passed. To this day, Patagonia is considered one of the most prominent B Corps.[116]

IS PATAGONIA UTOPIA?

Patagonia is clearly a mission-driven business. It is on a crusade that's very specific to its values and it isn't afraid of engaging in whatever aligns with that mission. It maintains an investment fund to drive sustainable innovation. It invests in companies that will be testing new materials that are more sustainable or that will improve the value chain. It is confident enough in its limited growth each year and its mission to have a sustainable business that has an impact on the world.

This could be a model for future businesses to follow. As *The Wall Street Journal* points out, "There's genuine shareholder value at the heart of many of Chouinard's ideals, which could carry over to all types of enterprise."[117] As society becomes more aware of each company's social contract, people can easily praise and criticise to potentially massive global audiences. This, in turn, can increase the pressure on governments and regulators to introduce socially aware legislation. If these concerns are already factored into the core business strategy, then it reduces the potential difficulties of being forced to adapt corporate practices to meet these expectations. More fulfilling, happier workplaces attract and retain better workers, who, in turn, design superior products and develop smarter strategies. The internal message is also positive, encouraging employees to feel valued and act as strong brand advocates, while also taking pride in the quality of the product and the exemplary position Patagonia has achieved

116 Certified B Corporation. "About B Corps." *BCorporation.Net.* January 2018. https://bcorporation.net/about-b-corps.

117 Seth Stevenson, "Patagonia's Founder Is America's Most Unlikely Business Guru," *The Wall Street Journal*, April 26, 2012. https://www.wsj.com/articles/SB10001424052702303513404577352221465986612

by challenging the established norms and staying aligned to its identity.

PART TWO

The Connecting Leader

"During times of universal deceit, telling the truth becomes a revolutionary act."

GEORGE ORWELL

How Corporate Leaders Connect Business with Society

Sustainability

Digital Revolution

THE **NEW NORMAL**

Hyper-Transparency

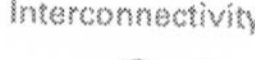

Media Anarchy

A NEW **SOCIAL CONTRACT**

Be Authentic with your stakeholders

Be Connected to your stakeholders

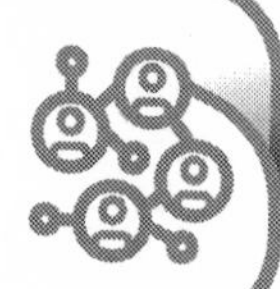

WELCOME **THE CONNECTING LEADER**

Authentic Leadership

Empowered Culture

Connected Intelligence

Economic Value + Social Value

CHAPTER FIVE

The Connecting Leader

NOW THAT WE HAVE DEFINED AND IDENTIFIED THE THREE types of authentic businesses, we are ready to move to the main actor who connects business with society. As we are beginning to see, companies need to adapt to the constant changes of the business environment, understand that reputations must emerge naturally from the company's identity and be able to identify and engage with the stakeholders who matter most to achieve the organisation's objectives. Here, I put forward the case to evolve the Corporate Affairs or Chief Communications Officer to an elevated role—defined here as the Connecting Leader—a position dedicated to connecting businesses with society. I will define the Connecting Leader's role, examine its key responsibilities and explore what makes a particular person well-suited for the role.

Connecting Leaders serve an increasingly important function as "Society Proxy." They bring the outside perspective in and apply a stakeholder lens to business risks and opportunities. Without a Connecting Leader bringing that perspective to the executive table, a business cannot be fully aligned with its context. The

Connecting Leader should be very much involved in providing strategic input to ensure the organisation's decisions are aligned with their identity (objectives, competence and character). As Richard Hamilton told me, "The job fundamentally is not inherently that difficult; what it requires is a mindset to be connected. Being connected is a state of mind that you live."

IT STARTS AT THE TOP

Who owns reputation? In a survey by *The Economist* published in 2005,[118] 84 percent of the respondents said they saw the CEO as the primary owner of reputation and reputational risk. Surveyed companies appeared to believe that only the Chief Executive should take ultimate responsibility for ensuring that all parties work in unison to protect reputation and manage crises. The survey also suggested that the CEO needed to be in charge of sensing the external perception of the organisation, a role backed by the communications function. Interviewees also emphasised the importance of the CEO's role in setting the right tone and standards of conduct to protect and enhance the company's reputation.

For a time, these assumptions were reasonable, but no longer. So much has changed that it has become crucial to assign a dedicated person to this role. The New Normal has created an environment that requires companies to engage with stakeholders and society more than before. The Executive needs someone in the "cabinet" helping to navigate the tricky path ahead of the business. The Connecting Leader is needed to step up and help the business stay aligned with society while still driving the business forward.

Matt Young, former Lloyds Banking Group Corporate Affairs

118 "Reputation: Risk of Risks," *The Economist Intelligence Unit*, 2005. https://databreachinsurancequote.com/wp-content/uploads/2014/10/Reputation-Risks.pdf

Director, puts it this way:[119] "The board are the guardians of the business; they are looking after its long-term future, and reputation has to be the first thing discussed at board level at every meeting. My job as the Corporate Affairs Director is to advise the board on reputational perceptions. I have to make the board aware that committing to take this action today might have these impacts. You know that a board understands the importance of reputation when they are prepared to leave an idea on the table for long-term sustainable earnings. They are prepared to leave money on the table and not do something in order to protect the reputation of the organisation."

While the CEO has a very important part to play in ensuring that reputation is well understood by the whole organisation, the effective CEO in today's business environment must give someone else responsibility for bringing the outside world into the organisation, connecting and aligning the internal organisation with the stakeholders' risks and opportunities and engaging with stakeholders to ensure that the company monitors changing beliefs and expectations. The most important contribution that the CEO can make is to create a role in the Executive Committee that has ultimate responsibility and authority—equal to the rest of the members of the Executive Committee—to ensure that the company makes decisions with full appreciation of its role in society and the reputational impact of that role. This is stressed by Claire Divver, who told me, "You need someone with Corporate Affairs responsibility on the Executive Committee with equal weight with the other members." Furthermore, Richard Woods asks, "Who is the customer for this function? The CEO, yes, but also the entire executive team and the Board of Directors. Managing reputation risk as a matter of policy enables executives to take on risk deliberately, not by accident and in a systematic and trans-

119 Helen Dunne."How Lloyds Banking Group is Restoring Trust," *CorpComms*, May 2014. https://www.corpcommsmagazine.co.uk/features-and-analysis/view/how-lloyds-banking-group-is-restoring-trust

parent fashion. As well, it extends the exercise of management discipline to a category of risk that is important to the board."

WHO IS THE CONNECTING LEADER?

The Connecting Leader is the "Society Proxy." The Connecting Leader's main responsibility is to ensure that the business understands its role in society. Good understanding, followed by actions that take into account such a role, will not only protect the company's reputation but also enhance it. The Connecting Leader accomplishes this by managing multidisciplinary, cross-functional teams that work closely with the company's stakeholders. He or she is well-placed to identify reputational issues and plant responses in broader strategy, operations and communications. The areas involved might include regulatory affairs, the general counsel, corporate communications, supply chain, marketing, employee relations, community relations and investor relations. As Nigel Fairbrass points out, "Although it's important that reputation is not simply outsourced to the Corporate Affairs team, it's equally important that there is accountability for strategic leadership on reputation round the management board table. This also argues strongly for a central function of deep specialists to fulfil that role."

Of all the functions that make up the organisation, no other is better placed to take the role of the Connecting Leader than the Corporate Affairs/Communications Director. The Corporate Affairs leader is one of the few, aside from the CEO, who has the perspective to see the multiple, and in many cases conflicting, business forces that are likely to have a reputational impact. As we will see in Chapter Nine, some companies are already putting Corporate Affairs Directors in an advisory capacity. However, this role must be completely embedded in the Executive Committee and the Board. The CEO must make this role a close partner who brings the outside perspective that other functions cannot bring. Failure to empower the Connecting Leader will keep the role overly tactical, short-termistic and detached from the core of the business, thus missing the opportunity to make the company more aligned with its stakeholders.

The Connecting Leader needs to lead with the truth of what is happening around the business and they must earn the right to be listened to by reporting strong facts. They need to have a thorough understanding of the business and what drives the stakeholders, which will vary from stakeholder to stakeholder. Ultimately, that means they need to be able to rely on intelligence from experts on regulation, investment, staff issues, media issues and so on. All functions of the business will question whatever this leader brings to light, so it is fundamental that every piece of advice is supported by intelligence. A successful Connecting Leader is the one who is able to make their organisation understand that reputations must emerge naturally from the company's identity before any specific tactics will work. Richard Hamilton told me he thinks that "Connecting Leaders are crucial to strategy implementation because through the connectedness, they bring a practical understanding of what needs to be done."

As we will see in Chapter Nine, many Corporate Affairs Directors in global businesses still play a tactical communications role and as one prominent Chairman of three FTSE 100 companies says, have been considered "the crisis management guys."[120] There has been some progress: the most recent FTSE 100 Group Corporate Communications/Affairs Director Survey disclosed that 51 percent of the FTSE 100 have appointed Corporate Affairs/Communications to their executive committees, up

120 Watson Helsby. "FTSE 100 Group Director of Corporate Communications/Affairs Survey 2016/17," *The Watson Helsby Report*. *2016*. http://www.watsonhelsby.co.uk/insights-and-publications/ftse-100-group-director-of-corporate-communicationsaffairs-survey-201617-results.

from 44 percent.[121] While these numbers might merit cautious optimism, they are not good enough. If anything, these numbers indicate a lack of understanding of the strategic importance of closer alignment with society among senior executives in global public companies. Simone Niven from Rio Tinto believes "the role of Corporate Affairs is to be strategic. We should be connecting the functions and joining the dots. We are in an almost unique position in a company, we can see the organisation through the eyes of those beyond the mine or factory gate. It is this perspective that connected companies increasingly value."

A Connecting Leader supports these efforts by harnessing the power of integrated intelligence as well as summoning the courage to take a seat at the table, explain what's going on outside the company and embed the social consciousness that we've talked about in previous chapters.

THE MULTIPLE HATS OF THE CONNECTING LEADER

For the Connecting Leader to succeed, they must be fully connected—inside and outside the organisation. In the remaining of this chapter, we will explore the five key roles that a Connecting Leader must play in any organisation: Outside-In agent, Internal Connector, External Connector, Communicator and Reputation Risk Manager.

THE OUTSIDE-IN AGENT

Our research over the past decade has shown that the majority of organisations fail to consider thoroughly how a certain initiative or decision will be perceived among multiple stakeholders. One

121 Watson Helsby, "Staying on the Front Foot: The Contribution of the Corporate Affairs Function to the Leadership of an Organisation," *The Watson Helsby Report*, http://www.watsonhelsby.co.uk/insights-and-publications/staying-on-the-front-foot.

critical function of the Connecting Leader is to change that, to bring the outside world in and demonstrate how the company's decisions will be perceived by stakeholders, particularly those who pose a risk to the business. The outside-in role also lets the Connecting Leader highlight the possible (and sometimes disastrous) unintended consequences of a particular course of action. In so doing, the Connecting Leader can drive discussions and actions that might otherwise be ignored.

Bringing the outside in is generally agreed to be the most important contribution the Connecting Leader can make to an organisation. It is the essential contribution that helps ensure that stakeholder expectations are heard and considered into most areas of strategic and operational decision-making.

But what constitutes the "outside view"? In the current business context, it includes the views of the company's key stakeholders—which might be politicians, regulators, investors, analysts, consumer groups and NGOs—as well as the wide range of issues that emerge from all forms of media. Not surprisingly, these views often conflict, due to the different expectations and demands from each stakeholder group; however, without the engagement and support of the key stakeholders, companies will find it hard to succeed in the long run.

As Richard Woods from Capital One shared with me:

> You need to understand both the internal business context and the external stakeholder context for the company. You also need to map how the interest groups within both of these contexts interact with each other. That is why this job requires a cross-functional team to be successful and why the leadership of this process should be centralized. The corporate affairs function is well positioned to take on this role.

The role of the leader is to convene people representing different

> stakeholders, integrate their input and synthesize it into a well-grounded risk assessment and a recommendation for action.
>
> The process begins with bringing together executives accountable for the company's relations with key stakeholder groups. Every company has this expertise in-house, represented by the heads of government affairs, regulatory affairs, community groups, media relations, employee relations and so on. What is needed is a process for collaboratively sizing the reputation risk associated with corporate decisions. Bringing the perspectives of various stakeholder groups together enables a picture to emerge of how these groups might interact and what the true size and nature of the risk is. Equally important is the institution to commit to systematically take these risks into account before the decision is made. This commitment should be founded in an enterprise risk management policy.

As we saw in Chapter Two, operating in the New Normal requires companies to understand the intersection between business, politics and social issues to be able to predict and establish a position and a narrative that keeps all important stakeholders in balance. Interconnectivity enables stakeholders to collude on issues of shared interest and create strong coalitions and campaigns that at best distract companies from their objectives, at worst hurt them to the core with quasi-irreparable damage creating severe value destruction. Each of the crises described earlier in the book did not happen by chance; rather, at the core of each of these crises, the parties involved failed to recognise that these issues would come to light and erode the company's or individual's reputation.

There is no other function that is better placed than the interface between the company and its external and internal (mainly employee) stakeholders. Without this role, it is almost impossible to integrate the external environment into the business. While in theory this makes absolute sense, the reality is that many companies are still unable to move away from an "inward looking" perspective that creates an echo-chamber effect and that reinforces the established assumptions formed over many years in the organisation.

The Connecting Leader should be encouraged to challenge the established assumptions or "institutionalised instinct," not with personal opinions but with well-founded intelligence that clearly demonstrates the emerging trends and informs or predicts as much as possible the outcomes of the decisions taken by the business in order to make a valuable contribution to the strategic debate.

As Claire Divver, Group Communications Director of BAE Systems, told me, "The most important quality in this job is judgment—the ability to understand different and complex points of view and to provide the Executive Committee with a coherent expression of what the outside world is expecting of our company. My job is to bring the outside world into the boardroom."

THE INTERNAL CONNECTOR

One of the distinguishing attributes of authentic businesses is their commitment to linking their behaviour, decisions and actions to their identity. In these organisations, the ability to connect the organisation with a consistent narrative and speak with a consistent voice to an increasingly diverse internal audience, across all brands and business units, is critical. The bigger the organisation and the more stakeholder interfaces and touchpoints it has, the bigger the risk to dilute the message and give the appearance of compromising behaviours. This is especially relevant for global organisations in which recognising cultural norms plays an important role in engaging the internal audiences.

While this is an arduous task, it should be the responsibility of the Connecting Leader to set the right tone and ensure that communications and behaviours of employees across the organisation are aligned with the overall purpose, values and agreed messaging. The challenge of how to connect the function to the different strands of an organisation—and to help those strands connect with each other—has prompted rethinking how to design function, including the balance between centralised and localised, and a move from generalist communications to "hybridising" with specific areas of the business.

Michael Sneed, from Johnson & Johnson, thinks that "Understanding stakeholders and protecting reputation is more art than science, and it really starts with co-ownership. Everybody at Johnson & Johnson plays a role in protecting our reputation and it takes a diversity of perspectives, a receptive environment and a supportive culture to ensure that the company is consistently making the right decisions for its stakeholders. For us, this comes in the form of our business partners often bringing us to the table to say, 'Hey, we're wrestling with this complicated decision and want to consider what it might mean to different stakeholders and for our reputation. Let's have a conversation.' To me, when you are part of the decision, and not just dealing with the result of the decision, that's success."

With the possession of the "connected" view, the Connecting Leader is in a unique position to provide the intelligence to the rest of the organisation regarding the reputational risks and opportunities that the business should be considering.

THE EXTERNAL CONNECTOR

Turn the Connecting Leader around 180 degrees and he or she will be looking outward again, this time with a focus on how all the external stakeholders are interconnected. The External Connector role seeks the same consistency of intent, message and understanding that the Internal Connector seeks, this time with a focus on how outside parties work with each other.

Engaging with stakeholders is crucial in an interconnected world. As the former Communications Director of a security services global company with more than 585,000 employees worldwide told us, "Companies should reflect internally the interconnected nature of stakeholders externally. The accessibility of information globally can turn your treatment of suppliers in one country into a potential consumer or political issue on the other side of the world. Ensuring that there is one orthodoxy of position and that relevant stakeholders are informed appropriately and timelessly is critically important to building and retaining trust."[122]

In an intangible economy, the quality of relationships with stakeholders is a key strategic component as well as a source of business risk and opportunity. Increasingly, government departments, company boards and non-executive directors are asking whether these stakeholders and the reputational risk or opportunity they represent are being managed with the same rigour as other critical business activities.

The consequences of failing to make this connection couldn't be clearer. As Nick Helsby from Watson Helsby, an executive-search company based in the UK, told me, "One Corporate Affairs Director we interviewed, whose company was unable to convince regulators to approve a transformational merger, said that a big lesson had been learned about the importance of effective and early engagement with government and regulators. CEOs must be cognizant of the issues relevant to their organisation and really understand the political context in which they are operating and therefore, need people who provide very good advice about how to engage and communicate with policy makers."[123]

Similarly, in "Staying on the Front Foot," a paper from Watson

---

122 Anonymous interview amongst Alberto and colleague

123 Watson Helsby, "Staying on the Front Foot: The Contribution of the Corporate Affairs Function to the Leadership of an Organisation," *The Watson Helsby Report*, http://www.watsonhelsby.co.uk/insights-and-publications/staying-on-the-front-foot.

Helsby, one unnamed Corporate Affairs Director states, "I've some experience of building excellent relationships with media and government in Westminster or Edinburgh, only to find that supply/ops colleagues or sales colleagues saw their role to beat up their own stakeholders in the same geography. These people were then somehow surprised when the press coverage or Whitehall gossip about their actions was negative."[124]

A paper from the UK's Department of Business, Energy and Industrial Strategy (DBEIS) proposing Corporate Governance Reform states the problem this way: "Many companies and their boards recognise the wider societal responsibilities that they have and the benefit they gain through wider engagement around their business activities. However, examples of poor corporate practice where the views and needs of key stakeholders—employees and workers, suppliers, customers and pension beneficiaries—have not been given appropriate consideration and have raised concerns about how well UK companies are taking into account the views of key corporate stakeholders."[125] Richard Hamilton formerly from KPMG believes that particularly "now that the green paper on corporate governance is about how you are involving employees (and other stakeholders) in your decision-making, you need to engage with your staff."

The same paper shows that over 240 respondents had a clear opinion on the specific question of whether the stakeholder voice should be strengthened. Of these, 210 (around 86 percent) agreed that the stakeholder voice should be strengthened, while only thirty-three (around 14 percent) disagreed. The DBEIS plan

---

124 Watson Helsby, "Staying on the Front Foot: The Contribution of the Corporate Affairs Function to the Leadership of an Organisation," *The Watson Helsby Report*, http://www.watsonhelsby.co.uk/insights-and-publications/staying-on-the-front-foot.

125 Department for Business, Energy & Industrial Strategy. *Corporate Governance Reform.* DBEIS, United Kingdom. 2017.

brought Corporate Governance Reform into effect on June 2018 to apply to company reporting going forward.[126]

The Connecting Leader should be uniquely placed to champion stakeholder engagement in a way that is aligned and consistent with the company's identity. When stakeholder relations are built with empathy, they create trust and goodwill, which helps to neutralise unforeseen negative reactions toward the organisation.

Consistency of stakeholder engagement is fundamental to maintaining the reputation of the organisation, be it across functions, business divisions, or geographies. To achieve this level of consistency, the Connecting Leader must be allowed to implement a stakeholder portfolio management model to engage with and establish equilibrium among the whole range of stakeholders who are key to the organisation. While each business has different stakeholder configurations, most should make sure they are managing their engagement with government, politicians, investors, analysts, communities, NGOs, media, consumer groups, opinion formers and any other key stakeholders.

Building a successful stakeholder portfolio is a complex task and one that requires deep understanding of stakeholder agendas and ability to weigh their significance to the overall business. To keep the stakeholder portfolio relevant and up-to-date, the Connecting Leader must continually identify new stakeholders and third parties with whom an organisation should build relationships in the future.

The Connecting Leader has the unique opportunity to encourage the rest of the business to engage honestly and transparently and in line with the company's identity. Simone Niven from Rio Tinto recognised the importance of long term partnerships "particularly with the communities in which we operate as well

126 Department for Business, Energy & Industrial Strategy. *Corporate Governance Reform.* DBEIS, United Kingdom. 2017.

as with governments. The social contract has always been really important. What has changed in the past couple of years is that we are now challenging ourselves to invest more work and resources into the way we engage with society."

When connecting externally, being inclusive is paramount. Richard Woods from Capital One argues that "the pool of influencers is expanding. 'Grass top' leaders remain important, but you also need to engage people at the grassroots level. Today's digital landscape not only rewards agility but inclusivity as well."

THE COMMUNICATOR

Traditionally, a key role of the Corporate Affairs or Chief Communications Officer has been managing the communications function and processes of the business, both internally and externally. This has included managing the communication channels with a wide range of stakeholders, including employees, shareholders, media, bloggers, influential members of the business community, the press, the community and the public.

For Lauren Day, Chief Communications Officer of Prudential Financial, "the communications function is a steward of the soul of the company. We understand the values of the company. We understand what's happening in the market and why. We directly engage with stakeholders of all kinds. And so we are well positioned to help develop and deploy the company's authentic voice to be relevant and purposeful on the issues that matter to stakeholders."

In the New Normal, the media relations landscape has changed from a model in which previously, the Communication Director interacted with a handful of journalists and influencers to having to monitor and understand a highly complex and "anarchic" media environment, including mitigating the effect of "fake news." In this context, the Connecting Leader mindset matters more than ever. By pinning all communication to the identity (objectives, character and competence) of the company, the Connecting Leader can ensure that he or she "owns the narrative" and can rebut the effects that fake news, half-truths, or misinformed opinion might have on the reputation of the company. When I talked with Ken Darby, Vice President of Communications and Government Relations at Thales, he told me, "If the communication executive today is not considered a strategic business partner, you can still get things done, but you're not showing the full value of communications to the organisation."

As emphasised in this chapter, the Communication Officer should have a holistic view, understanding both external and internal perspectives. This holistic view is necessary to ensure that the organisation is aligned with its brand and values. Consistency is key.

The Communications Director often faces challenges when trying to achieve consistency—for example, damage control: crises may cause damage to the organisation's reputation and cannot be predicted, so companies need to react fast when they occur. Communication is crucial in this process, as one CEO described: "I don't believe in crisis planning. I believe more in the right daily attitude; understanding how to behave and communicate. It should be part of communications management but also part of the overall management mindset and DNA." This CEO continued to explain how the communication officer plays a role in bridging the gap between board and stakeholders. For Richard Hamilton, "The role we're talking about is the ultimate insider-outsider; the job is to bring the outside in and find ways in which to develop and craft an architecture of messaging for the inside out. That requires somebody leading that role to understand that their job is not, perhaps as it might have been fifteen years ago, to develop a set of messages almost like it was a one-way conversation. There is a maelstrom of noise out there and you've got to find ways to cut through and get your message out."

An interesting perspective is presented by Richard Woods, who believes "Today, the company is one of the most trusted sources of information about itself. That's new. Not long ago, if you wanted to know about a company, you would rely on third parties—securities analysts and business or consumer reporters. Now, when people want to know about a company, the first place they go is to the company's web site. Therefore, company-generated content is key. Content that is fresh, relevant, factual and helpful enables companies to engage important constituencies at all levels. In a time when the reliability of so much web content is dubious, the company's voice is more persuasive than ever. The current environment favors companies who do a superb job in content development and curation. They've never had a stronger hand than today."

Corporate communication has evolved, too; while previously, communication would be about "broadcasting," today, it is about dialogue with key stakeholders. Claire Divver from BAE Systems confirms that: "We have done a lot of work with the chairman and the board who have been very supportive over the last five years of being more open and visible. We have adopted a much less formal corporate tone in the way that we talk to people. We are approaching communications as an opportunity to build a relationship and to start a dialogue. The other side of that [is] it's not just about talking but about listening actively."

THE REPUTATION RISK MANAGER

The Connecting Leader must also take on the role of Reputation Risk Manager—someone who looks at the risks the business is facing across products, sectors and clients with an eye toward heading off any actions that might potentially damage reputation.

When I sat down and spoke with Richard Woods from Capital One, whose role as Senior Vice President of Corporate Affairs included the duties of a reputation risk manager, he shared with us the process he developed within Capital One, a framework designed to connect the organization with reputational issues by creating an integrated approach to managing enterprise risk.

Capital One embraced this new framework by implementing a management discipline that recognises reputational risk as an integral part of business decision-making, much the same as credit risk or operating risk. This management process was designed to achieve four objectives:

- Address decisions made enterprise-wide
- Systematically engage product managers, line of business heads, members of the Executive Committee (C-Suite) and the board
- Adhere to auditable processes consistent with the bank's other risk-management programmes
- Produce measurable outcomes

Today, Capital One's formal Reputation Risk Management Programme has three foundational components:

- Enterprise Reputation Risk Policy: It holds the enterprise responsible to its board of directors for managing its affairs within a defined "risk appetite."
- Enterprise Reputation Risk Standard: It defines specific executive accountabilities and the processes to which the company must adhere in implementing the Policy, including the frequency and form of reporting to the company's internal and board risk committees. The Standard names a member of the Executive Committee as the "enterprise reputation risk steward," and the CCO is the "designated reputation risk executive."
- Business Line Procedures: It outlines the requirements that the business lines must apply in order to implement the enterprise-level standards.

Recognising early on that, to be successful, reputation assessment requires input from experts in stakeholder relations who are organised in functions outside of Corporate Affairs, Capital One formed a cross-functional team called the Reputation Risk Council composed of these experts and their peers in Corporate Affairs.

The Council is chaired by the CCO and is the body responsible for making assessments of enterprise-level reputation risk. Council members bring to this task decades of experience with their individual stakeholder groups as well as insights gleaned from opinion research, statistical trends in customer satisfaction and complaints, employee engagement scores and corporate reputation rankings.

To drive reputation risk considerations deep into the enterprise business lines, Corporate Affairs also designates a member of its team to be the reputation risk adviser to each business line so that they can take reputation risk into account at the earliest stages of product development.

The CCO submits a quarterly "enterprise reputation risk report" to members of the internal and board-level risk committees that marks trends in stakeholder group attitudes, details risks arising from each business line and summarises the enterprise's overall reputation risk exposure. The report in its entirety reflects the integrated view of the Council.

Occasionally, a proposed decision has the potential to create a level of reputational risk that exceeds enterprise risk appetite. In such cases, the Standard describes an "escalation path" and formal communication sequence that begins with the product manager, moves to the business line head and could include the members of the Executive Committee, the CEO and the board, depending on the circumstances.

Over the past ten years, Capital One's Reputation Risk Management Programme has made consideration of reputational risk a routine part of business decision-making. It has also systematised engagement with Capital One stakeholder experts, including members of the enterprise corporate communication team, at every level of the value hierarchy.

Richard Woods explained that "reputation risk management is a function that is mandated through a policy approved by the board of directors and applied across the enterprise. It is audited and treated no differently than other risk functions at the bank. It's operating requirements and output are reviewed annually by the board of directors." When discussing reputation risk pattern identification, Woods continued "reputation risks can bubble up from all over the place, so you need a systematic way of assessing these risks as they emerge. Taking measured risks is what business does all the time. But the company is better positioned if it knows what the fully-loaded risks of their decisions are and are prepared to address them if they become reality."

THE RIGHT ENVIRONMENT TO SUCCEED

Companies that operate in line with their identity invest in creating a more connected organisation across all stakeholders and functions; they are the ones that stay authentic and create more value. This can only be achieved when the company embeds the right leadership in the organisation, promotes an open and honest culture and obtains connected intelligence to engage with its stakeholders, rather than ignoring these groups or, even worse, antagonising them.

These three key components—Authentic Leadership, a Culture of Empowerment and Connected Intelligence are covered in the following chapters to provide a full understanding of what Connecting Leaders should look for in their organisations to foster a conducive environment to connect.

CHAPTER SIX

Authentic Leadership

NOW THAT WE HAVE DEFINED THE ROLE OF THE CONNECTING Leader, we will explore the concept of Authentic Leadership, the first of the three components that must be in place in the company to implement the Connecting Leader role successfully.

For a Connecting Leader to succeed, two key circumstances must meet. First, there must be recognition and support from the CEO and board for creating the Connecting Leader role. Second, the individual performing the Connecting Leader role must have the right leadership skills. The collision of these two circumstances is critical to the success of the role—i.e., an organisation might have a world-class, visionary CEO, but having a Connecting Leader with poor leadership skills will result in poor execution. Likewise, a competent Connecting Leader might find it highly frustrating operating in an environment that doesn't have an appreciation for the role. While this is an obvious point, our research shows that in many cases there is a lack of understanding of the value that the Corporate Affairs function can bring to the organisation and the role is limited to tactical activities. Michael

Sneed from Johnson & Johnson considers that "CEO support is the key. That person is the one who has the ability to connect your work across the enterprise and embed your priorities into the company's overall strategy. Without CEO support, the work is discrete, service-oriented, or exists in a silo, and by definition has limited impact. With CEO support, your contribution to growth can increase exponentially."

The New Normal has forced a high degree of collaboration between the executive/board and Corporate Affairs. Our research found a general trend toward greater involvement of the Corporate Affairs function in strategy and business planning. In the more highly regulated industries, where the bottom line impact of regulatory activity can be significant, business strategy is increasingly informed by political and regulatory issues. Simone Niven from Rio Tinto believes that "the number one driver of success for the function is to have a chief executive who really wants to lead and advocate the work we do in Corporate Affairs. With their endorsement, the team can start to influence decision-making right across the organisation."

The increasing demand for connection with society means that the current Corporate Affairs function is becoming more influential in the business. The function is having to learn to behave and operate like a business discipline and strategic function (rather than a specialist practice area) with implications for leadership and management skills, processes, systems, KPIs, etc. The leader must be able to demonstrate a real and deep understanding of the business they are leading and the people within the organisation. Relationship-building skills, along with the intellect and interpersonal skills to engage effectively with external stakeholders, will remain important, albeit with a demand for a higher level of sophistication. But the function needs to expand and strengthen its capability if it is to deliver the business benefits that will increasingly be expected of it.

Selecting the right leader to step in to the Connecting Leader role and ensuring that the organisation is developing the next generation of leaders is all the more challenging for one important reason: the nature and scope of the Connecting Leader is significantly different from other roles reporting to the CEO. The ability to assess whether aspiring executives can make the leap to the Connecting Leader role is critical to adopting this new business discipline.

What combination of leadership and technical capabilities, experience and aptitudes defines the highest-performing Connecting Leader? It's a question that CEOs will wrestle with and one that aspiring leaders will consider, too.

THE AUTHENTIC LEADER

In the New Normal, Authentic Leadership matters more than ever, but what are the traits that we can find in authentic leaders? They are genuine and believe in what they do, showing a willingness to be open to what they don't know and expressing their true feelings and emotions. Authentic Leadership also manifests by acting ethically, ensuring that words and actions match, showing that one serves a purpose beyond oneself, being confident and showing conviction in what one does and how it's done, and being able to articulate why the vision and direction are right for the organisation and those within it. These leaders exhibit self-awareness by being sensitive to the impact on others and being able to demonstrate a real and deep understanding of the business they are leading.

When I sat down and spoke with Michael Sneed from Johnson & Johnson, he shared the "connected" leadership framework at the pharmaceutical giant. Johnson & Johnson has four leadership imperatives: leaders that connect, leaders that shape, leaders that lead, and then, ultimately, leaders that deliver. "For us, leaders that connect is all about purpose. We have incredibly purpose-driven employees who don't just want to be told what to do, but want to be empowered to support the success of the overall organization. We want our leaders connecting our employees' passions to the opportunities we have today to change the trajectory of health for humanity."

When it comes to leaders that shape, Johnson & Johnson looks for leaders who can have an effective voice in how the organisation is successful or not. "At Johnson & Johnson, we are privileged to lead. We touch many aspects of healthcare in nearly all parts of the world, so fortunately, we have a prominent voice and loud megaphone. We need to use that for good. We want our leaders to use our expertise and our platform to shape our environment to create positive health impacts in the US and countries around the world."

In terms of leading as an actual imperative, it requires the leaders of Johnson & Johnson to lead in good times, but, more importantly, lead when there are difficult situations "where you have to make tough choices—for instance on where to invest and where not to invest—that impact the health of the business in both the short and long term. Real leadership requires conviction and values in making those difficult decisions, but they're essential to our overall health."

The last imperative is about leaders that deliver. In Johnson & Johnson they have to have leaders that "can deliver on the commitments that we've made as an organization to all of Our Credo stakeholders, including to serve the needs of patients, their families and healthcare providers around the world through our innovation pipeline, our communities by being an outstanding citizen, our own people through their development, and our shareholders by delivering a fair return."

There are many aspects that stand out about this leadership framework, but perhaps one that is key is that "it's tied not only to our business plan but also Our Credo," said Sneed.

One of the Connecting Leader's biggest contributions is to ensure that culture, strategy and purpose align. Proper alignment is the best foundation for constructive engagement with stakeholders based on a clear understanding of the company's purpose. To achieve this, Connecting Leaders must be willing and able to spark and continuously nurture two often little-developed insights in leadership: a deeper and broader understanding of the role of business in society and a profound appreciation of—and respect for—stakeholder concerns. This alignment contributes to ensuring that the whole enterprise lives its purpose—and properly expresses it.

In order to do that, the leader needs to map (and express in business language) the company's and sector's societal context as well as its cultural dynamics. This goes beyond a classic mapping and analysis of stakeholder concerns. Homing in on the company's reputation intelligence (see Chapter Eight) will allow the company to help the business leadership engage in strategic issues, develop a solid narrative and engagement plan, assure implementation and help the enterprise create space for the business to grow.

Why are some executives able to have a positive impact on the organisation while others cannot? The specific business context matters, as does how closely the individual fits the requirement of the role and the organisation's culture (as we will see in the next chapter); the clarity of the objectives for the role is also an influential factor. Furthermore, leaders who are most able to make the difference in their organisations have well-developed leadership capabilities and the ability to adapt and grow with the role in the business.

THREE KEY TRAITS

So what are the key traits that we should be looking for in authentic Connecting Leaders? Our research suggests three key traits: the ability to collaborate and influence, a strong capability for building teams and a deep understanding of and ability to anticipate stakeholder issues that will likely affect the business.

ABILITY TO COLLABORATE AND INFLUENCE ACROSS THE BUSINESS

Achieving the strategic objectives of the business requires that functional and business leaders collaborate in new ways to plan and execute key initiatives and remove barriers to change.

As seen in the previous chapter, it is essential that the Connecting Leader engages with the board of directors, having to anticipate the directors' concerns and perspectives on strategic issues, but also being able work with other functions of the business to obtain their "buy-in." During our research, many interviewees spoke of the need to invest time in building relationships throughout the company—strong internal relationships, together with a deep knowledge of the business.

In complex businesses like global public companies, the ability to collaborate and influence the CEO and other management team leaders is essential. It is far more difficult to influence and collaborate with executives outside of one's own functional domain who don't share the same language or perspective on the business. Connecting Leaders who excel in this area have a strong understanding of the drivers of the business and find ways to engage and build partnerships with their colleagues. These executives are also most likely to end up in the CEO's inner cabinet; they become a partner to the CEO and have a disproportionate impact on the senior team, the strategy and the broader organisation.

The Connecting Leader who lacks the ability to collaborate and influence risks becoming pigeonholed as the "communications" person or "crisis management" person. The inability to influence and collaborate across functions and business units within the first twelve to eighteen months can lead to failure in the role.

In some ways, this isn't a new skill. Professor Brian Uzzi explains what allowed Cosimo de' Medici to become de facto ruler of Florence for much of the Italian Renaissance. He exemplified a special leadership skill—the ability to get diverse teams of contending bankers, merchants and traders to collaborate effectively. How? He identified with each group's sentiments and mindset. With that understanding, he succeeded where others failed. He built new bridges of common purpose, resulting in a "team" that produced greater, more sustained economic, social and cultural value for all parties—and the broader society. Central to Cosimo's success was what Uzzi calls "multivocal leadership." Connecting Leaders have a similar role in building bridges of common purpose. As Richard Hamilton says, "You need to have people that have a broad view and can reach out to lots of people, internally; if you've got the skills to be connected, you will form the relationships with whoever you need to form them. You need to bring a degree of connection and evidence that you are connected—that's what matters."

Multivocal leadership is not about gaining technical proficiency in multiple areas—Cosimo knew banking but not trading, merchandising, or other areas of expertise and he didn't have the time to gain even nominal proficiency in other areas. Instead, multivocal leaders identify directly or vicariously through others with the experiences, mentalities and skills of a diverse set of people and they fluently broker communication among teammates to guide collaboration. This fluency across fields and cultures is essential to connect diverse, functional leaders who bring diverse perspectives.

Connecting Leaders need to understand, interpret and translate complex hard and soft issues affecting the business. The psychological concept of "perspective-taking" concerns the ability to place oneself effectively in another's shoes, gaining understanding and empathy for them.

As we will see in Chapter Eight, Connecting Leaders must also be proficient in using intelligence to arrive at the right decisions. Handling reputational intelligence means dealing with unprecedented volumes of information across many functions and stakeholders, as well as complex decisions regarding questions to ask, frameworks and tools to use and insights to seek.

A STRONG CAPABILITY FOR BUILDING TEAMS

Leadership and management skills, in a function that has historically not placed a great premium on these attributes, are becoming increasingly important as the practice matures into a critical senior level management function and the size of the team grows. Directors of Corporate Affairs in some global organisations now have to provide leadership to global teams of over 250 people, sometimes considerably more. This involves strategic leadership, capability building, governance, team building (successful teams are cohesive and coherent, and this is not easy to achieve on a global scale) and other leadership and management tasks. In many multinationals, it requires reporting at the board level with the same level of rigour and analysis as other corporate functions.

Being a function leader is a significant responsibility, and in most careers, one cannot progress beyond a certain level without sound management skills. But all too often, it comes second to the perceived day job—standard Corporate Affairs activities—which can affect functional coherence and prevent leaders from getting the extra discretionary effort out of people. Global public companies, which now pay more attention to the leadership capability with the Corporate Affairs function, are increasingly intolerant of people who are poor managers. When recruiting for a function lead, proven leadership ability has now become a key selection criterion.

A strong capability in building teams is a cornerstone for success in top functional leadership roles. These executives place the right people in the right roles and make tough decisions when necessary. They are also able to create a team of highly talented people who work together and are more than the sum of their parts. These leaders are great teachers who are gifted at asking "catalytic" questions, which allow their people to move forward in especially creative ways.

Lauren Day, Chief Communications Officer of Prudential Financial, deeply believes that strategy is a core skill of each team member and of the team as a whole, asking "what skills do you need to develop along the way, for yourself and for your organization, to be the leading strategic center for your company?" Day shared, "When I came to Prudential, I knew from experience that the one way to create a future-ready communications team was not to recreate something that already existed elsewhere. It was to focus on creating a culture of learning. What does this mean? This means a culture that revolves around the development of people: not only training in the technical skills we all need to learn to keep up with the trade, but also the abstract skills to increase the plasticity of the mind. Most senior communicators today were formed early in their careers as writers. The mastery of writing is difficult and rare and superb writing reveals deep subject matter knowledge and incisive analytical skill. But we have a lot more to do now in our jobs as strategists than just draft content. Good writing is table stakes."

When building a team to operate in the New Normal, Day looks for people who are able to develop and apply four different perspectives that represent tenets of good strategic counsel: an outside-in view, a portfolio view, a real-time view and a consequential view. She explains, "to bring an outside-in perspective to bear on business problems, we have to understand what is going on in the world and why. This means fluency in the natural, applied and social sciences, as well as expert knowledge of the business model of the industry. To bring a portfolio perspective to bear, we have to understand business strategies deeply, of course, but also understand the larger model and how a set of strategies complement one another. This means a fluency in products and services, in context with knowledge of the entire competitive landscape. To bring the real-time perspective and consequential perspective to bear, we have to master decision-making tools that require skills in data interpretation and digital technology." The talent strategy for Day's team is centered in helping individuals and teams hone the skills that underpin these four dimensions of applied thinking.

ANTICIPATE THE COMPANY'S ISSUES

Boards and stakeholders now expect more sophisticated and business-like interactions from the Corporate Affairs function. Internally, boards are increasingly looking for a more rigorous analysis of the reputational issues and risks to which their organisation is exposed. Relationships and access are important, but intelligence and robust analysis are now crucial requirements.

The Connecting Leader of today and of the future must possess a spectrum of knowledge and awareness that extends well beyond communications to include a broader understanding of the external environment and the increasingly complex stakeholder ecosystem. Different tools and skills are now required, such as scenario planning, forecasting, geopolitical risk analysis and economic modelling. CEOs, depending on their industry sector, will expect to be well briefed on broader geopolitical and socio-political issues that they may be required to discuss on public platforms. Richard Hamilton believes that businesses "need to have a view about how they see society developing, how they see an economy developing and how the company will develop within that. This is the point of connection. As you are imagining the role you play, you're not just a business with a return to shareholders but you are a player in society, and I think that's a whole new ballgame for businesses to realise. In that context, you need someone who has an ability to horizon scan, be connected and bring that back in a way that's relevant to the organisation."

To anticipate the company's issues and monitor the role of business in society, Connecting Leaders need intelligence covering key strategic stakeholders. Equipped with this intelligence, the leader can observe and act on the company's challenges and opportunities in their broader economic, political, social and cultural contexts and predict how these might affect stakeholder expectations. Adding "horizon scanning" helps gain an understanding of the issues that drive the agenda—not just policy and legislative changes but also demographic trends that are likely to influence government decisions both in the short and long terms. This information helps businesses prioritise their strategies and decide how to build advantages, create alliances, mitigate risks, enhance the reputation and become smarter market players. Good stakeholder intelligence also enables companies to shape a relevant narrative that expresses the company's purpose and links its role in society with its commercial offerings. Claire Divver believes that the Corporate Affairs role can bring the value of perspective. "It really is difficult for executives to rise above managing for the short-term challenges while thinking about how to manage the company so it's successful in the long term," she says. "Corporate Affairs can help to extend the time horizon that management is looking at by seeing the challenges ahead in the context of a much longer-term strategy."

The Connecting Leader's role includes understanding how

trends that are coming might affect the business. *Am I preparing this business for the future? Am I giving the CEO and business the input they need so that the business is always at the forefront of society?* Facilitating the alignment between society and its stakeholders with the business is one of the biggest contributions a Connecting Leader can make.

WHERE TO FIND AN AUTHENTIC CONNECTING LEADER

We've already outlined part of the answer to finding these leaders: they should bring the outside in and have Internal Connector, External Connector, communications and reputational risk management qualities. We've defined the profile of the role and the leadership traits that will allow that person to influence, build teams and use high-quality intelligence to foresee what's coming. But where do you find these leaders?

Richard Woods from Capital One thinks that diversity is key:

> One important dimension of diversity is diversity of outlook, experience and training. I have served in communications functions most of my career but came into it as an MBA, with a concentration in finance. Early in my career, I thought that it would have been helpful to have had experience in journalism, but my understanding of how capital markets worked was an advantage in a field filled with former journalists. At other points in my career, I was fortunate to work closely with experienced brand marketers. I learned an enormous amount from them. Overall, it's important for communication professionals to gain as much general business knowledge as they can so that they can integrate their unique perspective into the core business decision-making process. They're going to add a lot more value to the enterprise if they understand where other executives are coming from and how communication can help.

INSIDER OR OUTSIDER?

Should this exceptional leader come from within the organisation or outside it? We've done some research on whether a newcomer or someone internal is better suited for the role and the answer depends on which stage the company is in. If a company is performing well and is a stable and steady ship, it might work well to choose someone internal who understands the business, its inner workings and its culture. If, on the other hand, the company requires significant change and disruption in order to thrive, a different kind of leader is needed. In that case, an external hire is probably better.

Making the right leadership choice matters and it may not be the obvious choice. Consider the internal executive selected in a pharmaceutical company. She had not been in Corporate Affairs before and didn't have much previous exposure to the full breadth of stakeholders' issues. Nevertheless, she understood the culture, knew the business and was well-respected in the organisation. She demonstrated exceptional ability in conceptual thinking and in reading complex organisational and interpersonal dynamics; she understood everyone's underlying agenda and could see the political dynamics at play in a given situation. She leveraged these skills to help build alignment around key issues and kept everyone working effectively together. Colleagues went to her for advice because she had something valuable to say. Having quickly earned respect and credibility with the board, CEO and executive team, she has made a big early impact on the business. She had everything a Connecting Leader needs to be successful.

David Woolwine from Allstate, an insurance company, shared his experience with me. He said, "I've been with Allstate for thirty years. I started in communication and quickly moved into a management rotation programme for over twenty years with varying roles in business units covering everything from operations and customer experience to sales within the Allstate brand and other brands. The reason I was recruited for this job is because I did have a communications background and also had the understanding of how the business operated. The CCO at the time realised that if we are going to have somebody building this function, they should be somebody who understands the organisation and has contacts within the organisation to help decision-making."

On the other hand, Standard Chartered, a global bank headquartered in the UK, hired Tracey McDermott, the former Chief Executive of the Financial Conduct Authority, to become the Group Head of Corporate, Public and Regulatory Affairs as well as Brand and Marketing and to oversee all the stakeholder functions. To appoint someone who has not been a Corporate Affairs Director before but ultimately has the mindset to bring it all together was a bold and brave move by both parties. Tracey is still in the role and is making a positive impact on the business.

DEVELOP AUTHENTIC LEADERS

As organisations grow flatter and more diverse and as the global operating environment becomes increasingly more complex, there is a stronger demand for people who can lead at all levels of the company. The profile of top leaders is complex and evolving. Organisations need to develop fundamental leadership capabilities among critical individuals and teams—capabilities that include the ability to collaborate across boundaries, conceptualise new solutions, motivate diverse teams and develop the next generation of diverse and global leaders.

Authentic Leadership is needed to inspire team loyalty through expertise, vision and judgment. These leaders also have the responsibility to develop more leaders in their teams who are able to work collaboratively across the business. With organisations that continue to evolve rapidly beyond vertically integrated enterprises to networks and ecosystems, there is a need for leaders to work together in new ways, such as collaboration across generations, geographies, functions and internal and external teams.

However, are companies ready for the new type of leadership needed today? Many organisations may not be prepared to accept a new generation of leaders or even to build an environment that allows them to emerge. Yet, there are signs of change. Consider some of today's leaders: Google's Larry Page was thirty-eight at the time of his appointment; BAE Systems' Charles Woodburn was forty-six; and Uber's Dara Khosrowshahi was forty-eight. This new breed of CEOs is younger, more global and more digitally savvy than their predecessors. They have a better grasp of the New Normal and are better aligned with business's role in society today.

Organisations need to be prepared to look inside and ask who in the organisation is likely to be a true game changer, consider what type of leaders get promoted and conduct deep analysis of current leaders' conduct to identify and develop people with potential, wherever or whomever they may be. These are fundamental questions that will help companies identify and cultivate leadership talent that they will need to compete in today's New Normal.

Looking outside the conventional requirements for executives will help you find more leaders like this. This new perspective can also keep you from promoting someone into a senior functional leadership role before they are ready, a situation that often creates a value gap, where the person is not able to have full impact because they are less skilled at influencing, lack the necessary knowledge about the drivers of the business, or fail to build and empower a strong team. Without domain expertise or experience in the role, they may lack the confidence to engage in the debate about the critical issues facing the business, limiting the ability to be a true adviser to the executive team and the CEO.

The organisations that are the most adept at developing

succession-ready leaders identify high potential early, so they have the most options for moving people around. Job rotation, P&L experience and exposure to other functional areas and business units do help to prepare the leaders that the function requires. To achieve all of this, it is more than conceivable that companies will start to mentor and nurture their own Corporate Affairs people and recruit from within. People pursuing a career in Corporate Affairs will come from a wider range of disciplines than ever before, including business, legal, analyst and strategy backgrounds. New graduates entering the Corporate Affairs profession will need vast curiosity to gain a broad understanding of how societal issues affect businesses. Those who are already established in the industry will need to seek effective ways of updating their skills base to meet the changing requirements of the role.

LOOK FOR EXECUTIVE INTELLIGENCE

To identify competent senior leaders, the consultancy Spencer Stuart defines "executive intelligence" assessments that measure five key dimensions: business intelligence, contextual intelligence, interpersonal intelligence, learning intelligence and conceptual intelligence.[127]

Strong business intelligence manifests by applying analytical judgment in complex situations. Contextual intelligence refers to the ability to consider issues from an organisational or social perspective, whereas interpersonal intelligence conveys the ability to read and respond to others' emotional states to enable harmonious interactions. Conceptual intelligence enables leaders to produce big-picture insights from complex and disparate information.

127 C.Apffel, C.Kelly, R.Stark, R.Zhu. "Can they Make the Leap? What it Takes to Get to-and Succeed in- the Most Senior Functional Roles." *SpencerStuart*. March 2016. https://www.spencerstuart.com/research-and-insight/can-they-make-the-leap

Finally, a high degree of learning intelligence allows individuals to change how they think and act in light of new information.

These assessments are useful in evaluating the ability to apply analytical judgment, consider issues from an organisational and social perspective, read and respond to emotional states, bring in the big picture and act in light of new information. All are important traits for the Connecting Leader.

THINK GLOBALLY

Senior management in many businesses now engage with highly influential public individuals not only on national and international issues affecting their business but also regarding the wider corporate responsibility and societal agenda. Connecting Leaders who think globally engender a better appreciation of the broader environment in which the business operates and this perspective ensures that they are more likely to engage effectively and are thus well-suited for this role. Simone Niven from Rio Tinto considers it's a necessity to think in global terms, saying, "I spend most of my time on the ground in the markets with my teams. The more we understand the communities and the world in which we operate, the more value we can bring to the organisation. We also need to stay connected and never stop learning from our people, our peers, other industries and society at large."

Finally, Michael Sneed from Johnson & Johnson offers very sound advice: "Success lies in acting as a business partner and being able to articulate how reputation can help drive results for any particular segment, market, or geography. If you can demonstrate to your peers how reputation contributes to the overall growth of their business and their key accountabilities, you will find a lot of them embracing your partnership."

CHAPTER SEVEN

Freedom and Responsibility

WE'VE TALKED ABOUT THE IMPORTANCE OF AUTHENTIC Leadership, the support of leaders and the leadership skills of the Connecting Leader. But without a supportive company culture, a Connecting Leader would probably struggle to connect the business. Culture describes "the way things are done here." Specifically, it refers to the values, beliefs, behaviours, artefacts and reward systems that influence people's behaviour on a day-to-day basis. It should be driven by top leadership and become deeply embedded in the company through a myriad of processes, reward systems and behaviours. Culture brings together the implicit and explicit reward systems that define how the organisation works in practice, no matter what an organisational chart, business strategy, or corporate mission statement might say. We can also think of culture as the compass that points out what to do and how to communicate at any given time.

At Netflix, CEO Reed Hastings and former Chief Talent Officer Patty McCord redefined the norm for corporate culture within Silicon Valley. In 2009, McCord published a 127-slide

PowerPoint titled "Freedom and Responsibility," defining the corporate culture of Netflix, and it has been described as "the most important document to come out of the valley."[128]

Netflix offers an inspiring example. The Netflix culture presentation[129] has been downloaded more than 12 million times since 2009.[130] The presentation clearly describes a culture that combines high expectations with an engaging employee experience: generous corporate perks such as unlimited vacation, flexible work schedules and limited supervision, balanced with a strong focus on results and appreciation for the expected achievement.[131]

People find the Netflix approach to talent and culture compelling for a few reasons. The most obvious one is that Netflix has been really successful. The number of Netflix streaming subscribers has been constantly increasing over the years, surpassing the 100 million mark in the second quarter of 2017. All that aside, the approach is compelling because it derives from common sense.

McCord recounts two principles that shaped Netflix's philosophy: "The best thing you can do for employees is hire only 'A' players to work alongside them. Excellent colleagues trump everything else." The second principle is: "If we wanted only 'A' players on our team, we had to be willing to let go of people whose skills no longer fit, no matter how valuable their contributions had once been. Out of fairness to such people—and, frankly, to help us overcome our discomfort with discharging them—we learned to offer rich severance packages."

---

128 Gregory Ferenstein, "Read What Facebook's Sandberg Calls Maybe 'The Most Important Document Ever to Come out of the Valley,'" *TechCrunch*, January 31, 2013. https://techcrunch.com/2013/01/31/read-what-facebooks-sandberg-calls-maybe-the-most-important-document-ever-to-come-out-of-the-valley/

129 Netflix, "Netflix Culture: Freedom and Responsibility." Netflix. https://jobs.netflix.com/culture

130 Steve Henn, "How the Architect of Netflix's Innovative Culture Lost Her Job to the System," *Planet Money*, NPR, September 3, 2015. https://www.npr.org/2015/09/03/437291792/how-the-architect-of-netflixs-innovative-culture-lost-her-job-to-the-system

131 Patty McCord, "How Netflix Reinvented HR," *Harvard Business Review*, January–February 2014. https://hbr.org/2014/01/how-netflix-reinvented-hr

Furthermore, the culture at Netflix is based in five key tenets:

1. Hire, reward and tolerate only fully formed adults.
2. Tell the truth about performance.
3. Managers own the job of creating great teams.
4. Leaders own the job of creating the company culture.
5. Good talent managers think like businesspeople and innovators first and like HR people last.

This level of honesty and common sense is still rare in culture statements or people policies, which either come across overly friendly, phony and unauthentic or are overly rigid and driven largely by fear of litigation.

A culture that is not based on "personal responsibility" is a culture that fails to do the right thing. Looking back at Wells Fargo, we can see what happens when a culture is not based on "common sense" principles but rather on achieving business goals at the expense of the reputation of the company. In an article in *The Wall Street Journal* describing what caused the Wells Fargo debacle, the former CEO said that employees failed to honour the bank's culture: "They did not do the thing we asked, namely to 'put the customer first.'" As we saw earlier, Wells Fargo employees failed to behave ethically because the signals coming from management were less about putting the customer first and more about achieving targets, which drove the disreputable behaviour, costing the bank a fine of $1 billion in April 2018.

THE RIGHT CULTURE DRIVES SUCCESS

The right culture drives people's behaviour, innovation and the success of the business. In a survey by Deloitte University analysing employee trends, 82 percent of respondents consider culture to be a competitive advantage for any business.[132] When we look at culture, however, we need to look at it from a business perspective rather than a HR perspective. The CEO and the executive team (including the Connecting Leader) should take full responsibility for embodying the behaviours and cultural norms that define the organisation's culture, with HR supporting through measurement, process and infrastructure.

To a certain extent, due to its "intangible" nature, the concept of "culture" suffers a similar fate as "reputation," which is that it is not always well understood. Many organisations find it difficult to measure and even more difficult to actively influence it. Only 28 percent of the survey respondents believe they understand their culture well, while only 19 percent consider they have the "right culture."

In the New Normal, where all kinds of news travels instantaneously and an organisation's culture is both transparent and directly tied to its reputation, great companies consciously cultivate their culture. Many companies are proactively defining culture and issuing culture "manifestos." Culture is particularly important during times of great change and the disruptive nature of the New Normal creates an opportunity for companies to consider how the character of the company aligns with their identity and ensure that the company's artefacts and reward systems reflect that character. The Connecting Leader can provide invaluable input in partnership with the Chief People Officer to cultivate a culture of authenticity across the whole organisation.

The ideal culture for a Connecting Leader to succeed in his or her pursuit to connect business with society has four distinctive characteristics. That culture will:

---

132 "Global Human Capital Trends 2016," *Deloitte University Press*, 2016. https://www2.deloitte.com/insights/us/en/focus/human-capital-trends/2016.html

1. Implement a structure that enables contribution
2. Engage everybody with the mission
3. Promote ongoing learning
4. Monitor culture purposefully

A NETWORK OF TEAMS

The complex nature the Connecting Leader's work means it requires an organisational structure that allows fast flow of information and promotes flexible responses to the issues that affect an organisation. Hierarchically structured organisations were designed around traditional management thinking in which leaders "tell people what to do, set goals and create standards."[133] But in today's operating environment, the ability to quickly build, deploy, disband and reform teams is critical; employees need to be able to respond to and engage with multiple stakeholders and their emerging requests all the time.

This new type of organisation, which we call a "network of teams," moves beyond the concepts of the unwieldy 1960s-era matrix organisation. Hierarchical structures can be helpful, but their usefulness is limited in the New Normal. Small teams can deliver results faster, engage people better and stay closer to their mission.

Recently, we have even seen strictly hierarchical organisations like the military take a second look at the traditional structure. In his book *Team of Teams*, General Stanley McChrystal describes how the US military's hierarchical command and control structure hindered operational success during the early stages of the Iraq war.[134] After watching Al-Qaeda disrupt his army and win bat-

133 Stacia Sherman Garr, "High-impact Performance Management: Using Goals to Focus the 21st-Century Workforce," Bersin by Deloitte, 2014. https://legacy.bersin.com/uploadedfiles/12-17-14-HIPM-WWB.pdf

134 General Stanley McChrystal, *Team of Teams: New Rules of Engagement for a Complex World* (New York: Penguin Publishing Group, 2015).

tles, McChrystal's solution was dramatic: decentralise authority to highly trained and empowered teams and develop a real-time information and operations group to centralise information and provide all teams with real-time, accurate data about war activities everywhere. Wylie Rogers from The Tantalus Group told me he advocates that "central coordination can be helpful to help drive and measure change, to share best practices and ensure work is aligned to business strategy. Success largely depends on the culture of the company."

McChrystal did not change the formal structure of the military. Rather, he created a new structure that allowed for dynamism and flexibility within the overall organisational structure. This new structure enabled officers to quickly move from their administrative positions to mission-oriented projects for a set purpose, knowing that they would once again have a home to return to within the larger organisational structure after the mission was completed.

Connecting Leaders who adopt this new model of organisation—a "network of teams" with a high degree of empowerment, strong communication and rapid information flow—can engage teams across different regions and diverse stakeholders. This model is extremely useful because it does six things:

- Empowers teams to set their own goals and make their own decisions within the context of an overarching strategy or business plan, reversing the traditional structure of goal and performance management
- Replaces silos with an information and operations centre to share integrated information and identify connections between team activities and desired results
- Organises these teams around issues or stakeholder groups rather than business function
- Teaches and encourages people to work across teams, using

techniques like "liaison officers" (in the US military) that promote collaboration and job rotation to give teams a common understanding of each other
- Enables people to move from team to team as needed—similar to the way experts come together on Hollywood movie sets—and then ensures that people have a home to return to once a team-based project is done, which changes the concept of a "job description" to that of a "mission specialist" or "technical specialist"
- Shifts senior leaders into roles focused on planning, strategy, vision, culture and cross-team communication

There are a number of companies such as 3M, Nestlé and other innovative companies that are decentralised and use shared intelligence centres to help teams maintain alignment with overall business strategy.

Two major factors are driving this organisational structure change. First, the pressure to respond to stakeholder issues quickly, combined with a generally greater sense of empowerment among the workforce, is making small teams a more natural and productive way to work. Small teams can deliver results faster, engage people better and stay closer to their mission.

Second, digital tools help teams stay aligned. Today, teams can easily use web or mobile apps to share goals, keep up-to-date on stakeholder interactions and address stakeholder issues. Rather than having to communicate up and down the corporate pyramid, people can access information immediately, with companies using roles like "liaison officers" to make sure teams know what other teams are doing.

To prevent silos from impeding effectiveness and to improve collective thinking, intelligence centres help teams share common knowledge and see the relationships between elements. In the Iraq war, McChrystal set up an information centre to monitor seemingly random attacks by Al-Qaeda so that he could help teams see the patterns. Each team had a "liaison officer" responsible for communicating with other teams when information was needed quickly.

At Nestlé, a digital information centre brings together social network, TV and news information about all of Nestlé's food brands around the world to help product businesses see where a brand is succeeding or failing to gain traction. The corporate headquarters in Switzerland serves as a clearinghouse and strategic planning centre, distributing information everywhere and empowering the businesses to grow.

ENGAGE THE EMPLOYEES

According to the research report "The Missing Link" by Watson Helsby, "Employees are not only a significant strategic asset but potentially an organisation's greatest risk."[135] Employees' opinions and attitudes can create resistance to a fundamental strategic shift and can define, shape, enable and limit external reputations.

There's no doubt that a key stakeholder in any business is its people and authentic businesses cannot exist without a fully engaged team. In the New Normal, creating and maintaining that engagement requires constant effort and dedication, largely because of four conditions: First, there's a great deal of competition for talented millennials, many of whom are less loyal to organisations than ever before. Second, companies face a continued need to attract employees with technological and other specialised skills, as every company is digitising its business. Third, as we have seen, an organisation's reputation is now open and transparent, so job candidates can easily see if a company is a great place to work. Finally, employee demands are changing and

---

135 Watson Helsby, "The Missing Link." Watson Helsby. 2018. http://www.watsonhelsby.co.uk/assets/files/2018_04_ExecSummary_The_Missing_Link_Watson_Helsby_Research.pdf

today's workforce places a higher premium on flexibility, creativity and purpose at work. Nigel Fairbrass from Eterna Partners believes that "new entrants to the workforce over the coming years are likely to have a very different view on the role of enterprise, its responsibilities and its attractions as an employer. The values and culture of organisations will be of much greater importance in attracting and retaining talent than position or profitability, and to a generation already comfortable with astonishing levels of transparency at a personal level, they will expect companies to embrace the same openness and accessibility."

So how can the Connecting Leader support the Chief People Officer in ensuring great employee engagement? By working closely with the Chief People Officer and with the use of ongoing intelligence, they can devise engagement strategies based on real intelligence. A new generation of "pulse" survey tools and open anonymous feedback systems can allow employees to rate managers, executives and just about everything else at work on a near-real-time basis. The thoughtful use of such tools can create a true "listening environment" for employees while giving leaders critical insight into what is working and what's not working in the company.[136]

The movement toward this "always on," feedback-based approach to engagement is growing rapidly, disrupting traditional models of measuring and managing employee engagement. A number of companies are adapting to more complex employee demands by listening more closely, trying new approaches and actively addressing operational problems.[137]

---

136 Josh Bersin, "Feedback Is the Killer App: A New Market and Management Model Emerges," *Forbes*, August 26, 2015. https://www.forbes.com/sites/joshbersin/2015/08/26/employee-feedback-is-the-killer-app-a-new-market-emerges/#12107f135edf

137 Josh Bersin, "Feedback Is the Killer App: A New Market and Management Model Emerges," *Forbes*, August 26, 2015. https://www.forbes.com/sites/joshbersin/2015/08/26/employee-feedback-is-the-killer-app-a-new-market-emerges/#12107f135edf

PROMOTE ONGOING LEARNING

In today's highly competitive global economy and intensely competitive talent market, the C-suite clearly understands that companies that do not constantly upgrade skills and rapidly build leaders will not be able to execute their business plans. In today's business environment, learning is an essential tool for engaging employees, attracting and retaining top talent and developing long-term leadership for the company.

Employees at all levels now recognise that "the learning curve is the earning curve," and they are demanding access to dynamic learning opportunities that fit their individual needs and schedules.[138] Employees need to learn how to learn and the company can support that by providing access to resources, tools and connections that enable them to do their jobs and build their careers better. Lauren Day from Prudential believes that "by creating a culture of learning and collaboration, the talent will come to you. Smart people want to be around other smart people. Collaborative people want to be around other collaborators. If they are isolated or bored, they're disengaged. So by creating a university-like atmosphere, you build the culture that attracts the kind of people you want. The kind of people that the profession needs and the kind of people that the world needs. When you add the fact that communications, as a discipline, lets you engage with so many subject matter areas at once and offers natural exposure to senior leaders across the company, I can't imagine that ambitious new college graduates will hesitate to sign up for a role in communications before they sign up for investment banking or software engineering."

Thanks to systems that enable self-serve career development, staff are now being empowered to access subject-matter special-

---

138 Josh Bersin, "Spending on Corporate Training Soars: Employee Capabilities Now a Priority," *Forbes*, February 2014. https://www.forbes.com/sites/joshbersin/2014/02/04/the-recovery-arrives-corporate-training-spend-skyrockets/#2c110316c5a7

ists to curate their own learning "playlists," mixing and matching internal and external learning content from a variety of sources and formats. Articles, MOOCs (Massive Open Online Courses), podcasts and webinars can all be woven together into a personalised learning experience to help employees develop the skills they want to focus on.

MONITOR CULTURE PURPOSEFULLY

eBay is relying on new company values to make its envisioned culture a reality with more than just words. eBay's CEO declared himself to be the "Chief Culture Officer" to emphasise his personal commitment to driving change. On the first day of the new company, he introduced a refreshed company purpose and five new values intended to create a more brand-focused, inventive and bold work environment. The value statements are being monitored using a quantitative approach: eBay's team of organisational development experts and data scientists actively measures the strength and adoption of these new values, regularly surveying eBay employees on over fifty cultural attributes that are mapped to the five recently formulated values and conducting employee engagement surveys. These data are then combined with operational metrics to assess the extent to which compliance with cultural values impacts the business.

To compare the internal view—that of eBay's employees—with an external view, the analysts also conduct both thematic and natural-language analysis on news articles and Glassdoor content, to gain a data-driven understanding of the ways that people discuss eBay's culture in the open market. This strong effort has enabled eBay to quantify elements of its culture and gain a more accurate understanding of how people both inside and outside the company view it.

A NECESSARY PARTNERSHIP

Research by Watson Helsby shows that CEOs and business leaders more broadly, still devote more time to external stakeholders. However, this ignores a key reality and that is that a company's culture is now very visible from the outside and many external stakeholders will make judgments and decisions based on what they see or hear about its culture.

Thus, the internal brand and the external brand are now virtually indivisible in the New Normal. If culture and employee experience are not positive, it will have a negative impact on key stakeholder perception. Therefore, it makes sense for the Chief People Officer to form a strong partnership with the Connecting Leader to bring alignment between the internal and the external view.

CHAPTER EIGHT

Connected Intelligence

IN ADDITION TO AUTHENTIC LEADERSHIP AND A CULTURE of Freedom and Responsibility, every Connecting Leader must have in place sound and trustworthy Connected Intelligence. Access to connected intelligence enables the Connecting Leader to bring the outside-in view, to align the business internally to respond to and influence reputational issues and opportunities and to understand and connect with external stakeholders.

Businesses have always relied on intelligence, but Connecting Leaders in the New Normal need a new kind of intelligence covering many new dimensions. The tools and methods available from traditional vendors were not designed with an understanding of the new context and as we have seen, the world has moved on a great deal over the last ten years. Traditional approaches are no longer valid and companies are better off adopting an innovative, data-rich, integrated approach.

What does this new kind of integrated intelligence look like? It has to be simple and relevant in addition to providing decision-ready insight to engage and lead in all matters related to stakeholder issues. The key to obtaining connected intelligence is the ability to integrate business, stakeholder and media intelligence to understand and connect with the company's main stakeholders.

Connected intelligence brings together other functions, facilitates dialogue and leads to informed decisions and actions. It allows the Connecting Leader team to sit at a command centre and support teams whose job is to connect with the key strategic stakeholder groups, to have greater control and consistency over how the company's culture and communication is consistent with the company's identity. Michael Sneed from Johnson & Johnson shared his experience with me. "We have approached reputation intelligence by developing a centre of excellence to consolidate our best thinking and serve our whole organisation. We've found this approach gives us greater consistency to ensure all aspects of our business are monitoring and analyzing reputation in similar ways, and creates far greater quality and consistency."

THE TRADITIONAL WAY

One of the qualities the Connecting Leader must have is the ability to develop a deep understanding of the insight and intelligence obtained. Not every leader looks at the data this way. Nearly all executives (96 percent) admit they have previously discounted data they don't understand.[139] That's unfortunate, because the benefits of unlocking data's potential to guide, validate, or challenge instincts can inspire greater confidence and expedite decision-making. Based on PwC's Global Data and Analytics Survey,[140] executives from companies that have changed the way

139 "Global Data and Analytics Survey 2016: Big Decisions™," *PwC* (2016). https://www.pwc.com/us/en/services/consulting/analytics/big-decision-survey.html

140 "Global Data and Analytics Survey 2016: Big Decisions™," *PwC* (2016). https://www.pwc.com/us/en/services/consulting/analytics/big-decision-survey.html

they make their biggest decisions as a result of data and analytics are nearly three times as likely to report significant improvements in strategic decision-making as those from companies that have not done so.

Typically, Corporate Affairs leaders have relied on conventional media and social media monitoring, along with output- and outtake-based media analysis, periodic customer satisfaction surveys, employee-engagement surveys, investor sentiment interviews and other opinion leaders' research. However, in my experience, few venture beyond the conventional metrics used to measure the (output-based) activity produced by the communications and Corporate Affairs functions.

For wider "reputation research," companies commission a "deep dive" analysis of the company's scores on a number of reputation attributes, while also looking at competitors using the same measure, but these tools offer limited insight into what stakeholders think and feel about a company. They provide only a tactical analysis that's often incomplete and disconnected. The added challenge of measuring reputation this way is that it is a bit ad hoc and inefficient and it can lead to more confusion. In many cases, these tools fail to address the "so what?" question. While these tools might bring clarity about *what* is happening, more often than not, they fall short of explaining *why* it is happening and *how* it affects the business. With only fragmented, low-quality analysis available, companies and their executives often resort to instinct or intuition for reputation-related decisions.

Some leaders have excellent instincts, but it's simply not efficient or effective to rely on those instincts alone in today's always-on and interconnected environment. The ad hoc, inefficient approach often leads to more confusion, not less. Today, leaders need to cast their nets wider and deeper and then scrutinise their catch carefully. Thanks to today's technology and the extensive academic research carried out over the last twenty-five years in reputation modelling and measurement, a more connected and efficient approach is possible. Whether you can successfully adopt such a system is highly dependent on how well your key executives understand and appreciate the topic of reputation as a corporate value enhancer, as well as how ready they are to adopt reputation intelligence as a crucial input for the company's decision-making.

OUTPUTS, OUTTAKES AND OUTCOMES

One of the most important contributions of the Connecting Leader to the business is understanding and communicating to the rest of the business the impact that the company's activities have on the members of society and stakeholders. Without sound intelligence, companies might be guessing more than knowing what's the right thing to do. Most of the traditional measurement models have mainly focused on measuring media activity, which, while important, is a very small component of fully understanding whether reputation is an enhancer or destroyer of corporate value. What's surprising is that many communications teams still report media activity as a key metric up to the executive level. The CEO should be much more interested in obtaining intelligence that illustrates how stakeholder perception impacts business goals and value creation.

One of the biggest challenges the Connecting Leader is likely to face is the implementation of better intelligence, partly because much of the intelligence is found in multiple sources and is rather disjointed. This requires the move from output and outtakes metrics to outcomes when presenting meaningful intelligence to the rest of the company. To illustrate this point, let's look at how this shift might play out in the communications department (which should be part of the Connecting Leader's team).

MEDIA OUTPUTS

Media outputs measure effort or "movement," rather than "achievement." Similarly, media teams are often tasked with producing a certain number of pieces of content per day. Measures like this can answer simple questions, like, "Did the team do their work on time, within budget and in line with the objective or message?" They offer only a very basic assessment of a team's performance, yet they are still a major part of the measurement dashboard in many companies, perhaps because they are easy to report. Management, however, often finds these reports unsatisfying because they don't answer the key question: how does the output impact the business?

MEDIA OUTTAKES

Media outtakes measure the direct results of the communications team's efforts, such as impressions, engagement and visibility. They tell you how many press releases you sent out and how many people are engaging. Outtake metrics are often more informative and, thus, preferable to output metrics, because they offer management a more nuanced view of how much of an impression they are making with the brand's marketing. For instance, you can learn a lot from measuring social media engagement, where outtake figures encapsulate a lot of other information about how the content has performed. Such data is often quite informative—knowing how many people reacted to posts, without promotion, provides a snapshot of the overall quality, relevance and shareability of the team's work.

OUTCOME METRICS

The most important metrics for lasting success, however, are outcome metrics, which report on the actions stakeholders took as a result of media activity. Outcome metrics ask, "What change did the efforts make in the real world?" Answering this question might require finding out whether customer loyalty for the brand improved—by comparing it against the Net Promoter Score (NPS), for instance—or asking whether there was an increase in sales of a particular product as a result of the stakeholders' activities. These metrics are much more difficult to obtain than media outputs and outtakes and as a result, they are much less frequently part of a media team's KPIs—but they are far more meaningful to management.

The Connecting Leader knows that to drive change within the organisation, they need to embrace the journey from observations to information, from information to insights, from insights to decisions and actions, and from decisions to outcomes.

IMPLEMENTING A DATA-SCIENCE APPROACH

We have seen that leaders often rely on gut instinct to guide them—they use what we think of as the "art" of strategic decision-making. But what about the "science" side of the equation: data and analytics? Consider that 85 percent of CEOs told PwC that data and analytics create value for their organisations.[141] How can the Connecting Leader realise that value? One way is to ensure reputation intelligence is used as input for all strategic decision-making. Using intelligence in this way will drive change in the organisation that aligns the business more closely with its stakeholders. This type of decision—done with confidence, clarity and agility—can only happen through a combination of art and science.

To obtain decision-ready reputation intelligence, the Connecting Leader should invest in creating a data and analysis team

141 PwC. "Seizing the Information Advantage". PwC, Iron Mountain. (September 2015). https://www.pwc.es/es/publicaciones/tecnologia/assets/Seizing-The-Information-Advantage.pdf

that understands data's possibilities and will adopt the framework below to challenge the business in four areas.

DISCOVERY: OBSERVATIONS TO INFORMATION—THE WHAT

This first step mainly involves understanding the "what," with questions such as: *What is my reputation among my stakeholders? What are my stakeholders saying about me? What are the issues that matter to them?*

Discovery involves understanding the possible uses for internal and external inputs. It requires judgment about what information would be most valuable and relevant to the business. It also requires the freedom to experiment and a commitment to persistent scanning for available data.

INSIGHTS: INFORMATION TO INSIGHTS—THE WHY

In the second step, we aim to gain an understanding of the "why," with questions such as: *Why do I have this reputation? Why is my reputation better or worse than that of my competition? Why is my reputation "value-creating" or "value-destroying"?*

The Connecting Leader must bring data scientists and experts to the department. Moving from data collection to developing insights requires applying new techniques to existing and new data to generate insights. Creating a test-and-learn environment for continuously harnessing the insights gained leads to decision-ready insight.

ACTIONS: INSIGHT TO DECISIONS AND ACTIONS—THE "DO IT"

The third step involves taking actions based on the connected intelligence gathered in steps one and two. With the support of the two previous steps, the Connecting Leader can present options for reputation-enhancing actions to the rest of the executive team.

OUTCOMES: DECISIONS AND ACTIONS TO OUTCOMES—THE HOW

The final step involves gaining an understanding of questions such as: *How do my actions affect the business? Are these decisions value-creating? Are these decisions taking me closer to my business goals? Are they getting me closer to delivering on my Social Contract obligations?*

This includes creating a continuous feedback loop that analyses how the decisions that have been taken impact the business.

MADE TO MEASURE

Developing a robust, high-quality and up-to-date Connected Intelligence System (CIS) is complex, as it involves the integration of multiple and varied datasets across multiple stakeholders and regions. However, if the Connecting Leader is to be the "Society Proxy" of the business, he or she must incorporate this discipline in the function. The alternative is to continue using disjointed and ad hoc intelligence, which will affect the value created by the function and the readiness of the business to exploit opportunities. This will ultimately cause a loss of competitive advantage.

Companies are sometimes tempted to implement off-the-shelf dashboards or standard reputation frameworks that ignore the importance of contextualising the intelligence system within the value drivers of the business. Without this contextualisation, the value and quality of the intelligence diminishes and they end up with a "square peg, round hole" situation, which then pushes the leader to rely more on instinct than data. Buying a ready-made system vs designing a custom Connected Intelligence System will lead to very different results. The latter gives a much better fit.

When ready to sponsor a Connected Intelligence System, the first step is always to determine the purpose of the system. If the system is to provide decision-ready insight on the company's reputational matters, it must be based on the stakeholder-engagement strategy that the company has adopted.

A custom intelligence system must be able to compare the company against competitors, in the sector as a whole, as well as within the cultural norms of each country where the company operates, in order to allow the organisation to benchmark its reputation and contextualise its performance. Analysing all of the above requires integrating vast amounts of internal and external sources (e.g., perception studies, surveys, traditional, digital, social media, broadcast) and covering multiple stakeholders (e.g., customers, regulators, investors, employees, media, communities and others) to uncover the issues related to a particular stakeholder's perspective and provide an integrated and consistent view across all the stakeholders.

Connected Intelligence Systems must be completely tailored to the reputational framework of the business and offer the flexibility to adapt to changes in the stakeholder landscape in real time. The flexibility should also allow leaders to view multiple "slicing and dicing" variations of the datasets, in a variety of frequencies—real time, daily, weekly, monthly and annually.

The intelligence obtained must have the ability to answer multiple what, why and how questions, such as those we examined earlier in the chapter. This level of analysis and intelligence promotes effective comparisons and helps companies avoid ignoring potential issues or performance gaps. The analysis provides a starting point for an objective quantification of reputational risks. The company can assess the probability and financial cost of potential reputational events—like consumer boycotts or forced operations closures, for instance—and then prioritise those risks and implement the measures needed to keep them at bay.

Equipped with this intelligence, the Connecting Leader can advise senior management, functional heads and the board of directors regarding the implications of the company's decisions. He or she can also provide a perspective on the reputational risks and opportunities that the company faces across different markets and stakeholders that will inform the business of the actions that should be taken as well as bring clarity regarding the expected outcome from such actions.

Achieving the right level of intelligence eliminates guesswork; however, some crises are unforeseeable. If the system is too rigid, it might be unable to understand that a particular crisis is emerging. A good embedded system based on the company's identity and its roots will ensure that responses to issues will arise naturally from the culture of the business.

THE CONNECTED INTELLIGENCE SYSTEM (CIS)

Now that we have established that an action-based integrated intelligence system is required to allow the Connecting Leader to illuminate the reputational risks and opportunities that the company is facing, let's explore in more detail what the CIS looks like.

The CIS should be able to identify both real-time and long-range issues that the organisation faces. As we have seen, these issues emerge from the different perceptions of the complex universe of stakeholders and for global public companies, that also involves multiple countries or jurisdictions. The system must have three key components:

- Reputation Inputs (data)
- Reputation Intelligence Platform (technology-enabled)
- Reputation Intelligence Analyst (human)

REPUTATION INPUTS

The CIS must integrate two different data sets: Solicited Input and Unsolicited Input. The latter is divided into three categories: Influencing Agents, Amplifying Agents and Emerging Noise.

Solicited Input

Solicited Input comes from sources where stakeholders have directly provided their opinion on the company and its competitors and it is essentially "what people say when you are in the room." Even when Solicited Input is provided anonymously, the form of the question can colour the response. Additionally, Solicited Input might not to be as timely as Unsolicited Input.

This data can be helpful, though, and should be sourced both internally and externally to cover the company's interactions with stakeholders. For instance, the IR department will provide the share register and perception studies of the main investors and analysts; Marketing will provide a variety of customer insight, brand tracking studies and NPS; the HR department will access regular employee surveys, employee engagement activity and employee communication forums, such as Yammer; Supply Chain will have access to supplier surveys or the inventory-turnover ratio; and the regulatory function will have access to regulator meeting minutes and perception studies.

Where data gaps exist, the company should commission primary research externally or instruct the functional heads to commission the data from internal resources.

Unsolicited Input

Unsolicited Input refers to content related to the company from publicly available sources, such as traditional media, social media, broadcast, analyst notes, financial data, consumer forums and publicly available survey results. This is similar to me listening to what you're saying when I'm *not* in the room.

This type of input is split into the following three categories.

- **Influencing Agents:** Influential individuals, organisations, media, or sector bodies have the ability to shape an agenda. Influencing agents might be key opinion leaders, journalists, politicians, or other prominent individuals who represent the different stakeholders. These individuals have an opinion about your organisation and if they are vocal about it, they have the ability to shape an agenda related to issues that matter to the company.
- **Amplifying Agents:** Amplifiers are entities that have the ability to broadcast more widely. A newspaper like *The Wall Street Journal* can function as both an Influencing Agent and an Amplifying Agent, for example. When the *WSJ* article gets retweeted on Twitter, it has an additional amplifying effect.

- **Emerging Noise:** This is content that might not be fully related to the current issues and does not have the same influencing or amplifying quality as the other two categories but nevertheless might carry the signal of emerging issues that are buried in the long tail of content related to the company or its sector.

Within a CIS, Unsolicited Input can inform Solicited Input, creating a symbiotic relationship between the two types. Similarly, each type of Unsolicited Input informs the others; if Emerging Noise points to a possible political scandal and it gets traction with Influencing and Amplifying agents, it's likely to become a problem, as we saw in the case of Harvey Weinstein earlier in the book.

As we have seen, stakeholder perceptions are shaped by direct experience with the organisation as well as via a series of indirect proxies including media, opinion leader interactions and policies. The CIS must allow leaders to monitor the big picture as well as emerging local issues. That means that when constructing a CIS, the Connecting Leader must consider how to integrate direct experience with indirect proxies and normalised data sets (solicited and unsolicited) to obtain a 360-degree view of the multiple reputations of the company across multiple countries. Integration of these datasets must be tailored to the company to consider different weightings applicable to stakeholders, issues, sources and regions.

Comparing Solicited and Unsolicited Inputs

The resulting platform monitors and analyses content from across the globe in multiple formats and languages. The process of making meaningful comparisons between Solicited and Unsolicited inputs requires the following steps:

- With the solicited and unsolicited data collected, in addition to identifying reputation drivers and KPIs, this intelligence should be used to configure the real-time reputation intelligence platform.
- The platform should be configured to monitor and analyse entities in a number of different ways, using a sophisticated language pattern-matching approach, combined with source recognition and entity self-identification. Elements include companies, issues, business units, stakeholders, reputation drivers, regions, countries and cities.
- A reputation intelligence analyst should use the findings of the unsolicited data to configure specific profiles for each of the different country stakeholders. This approach helps to create a unique linguistic fingerprint of overlapping search terms, sources and identifiers, which will pinpoint content relevant to each group.
- Once content is identified for each stakeholder in each region, it should then be passed through the "reputation analysis" algorithm of the platform. The algorithm assesses the reputational impact of each piece of content with regard to the entity being tracked.

Combining Solicited Input (to understand the key issues and drivers of reputation across multiple stakeholders) with Unsolicited Input (enabling real-time monitoring and analysis of shifting stakeholder perceptions over time) provides a new integrated approach to obtaining connected reputation intelligence.

THE REPUTATION INTELLIGENCE PLATFORM

The real-time platform is designed to carry out monitoring and analysis to provide tailored multichannel, multilanguage, multistakeholder intelligence. Such a platform gathers data and processes it in real time, covering many millions of varied data sources and types.

MONITORING

The platform should collect Unsolicited Input data from every region, with coverage across print, online, broadcast and social channels in real time, 24/7. Not all sources are born equal, so it is important that the platform take into consideration how many people are likely to see the content and how trusted the source is, as well as the likely reader recall of the information. This can be achieved by automatically classifying content as to whether it is coming from an Influencing Agent or an Amplifying Agent or is Emerging Noise.

ANALYSIS

Once the data has been collected, the next step is to assess what is being discussed in each piece of content, with the help of Natural Language Processing (NLP) techniques. NLP allows a language-pattern-matching system to automatically assign results to a number of different categories. These categories include company, sector, region, stakeholder, issue, reputation driver and many more. A robust system should be able to match 500,000+ entities every second using this approach.

Each piece of content should be categorised in a variety of ways, including audience, frequency of publication, sentiment and amplification. This is a crucial methodological strength of the platform, as it will enable reputation to be viewed through different lenses. All of the processes and calculations described thus far are designed to create a highly nuanced, near-real-time reputation score split by stakeholder, region, reputation driver, issue and many other parameters.

As previously discussed, reputation is a relative concept formed and owned by stakeholders over time. The real value of a reputation score is as a benchmark for the company with a particular stakeholder group in a particular region, relative to its historic performance over time and also versus its peer group. This benchmarking gives the score both for context and actionability. When I spoke with Peter Mitic, Professor of Computer Science at University College in London, he told me he has carried out extensive research in reputation measurement over the years. He believes that "it's important to recognise that every reputation score that arrives tells its own story and that cumulatively the reputation scores show how that story progresses with time. The task, then, is to act on that information. If the cumulative reputation is downward trending, find out what is going wrong and try to fix it. If the cumulative reputation is upward trending, that is good news, but you should still find out why. Remember that instances of negative reputation are much harder to put right than instances of positive reputation are to put wrong."

THE REPUTATION INTELLIGENCE ANALYST

As we have seen, building a CIS can get complicated amidst the different variables and nuances that might be taken into account.

While the platform plays a critical role in data crunching and analysing data, if the goal is to obtain decision-ready intelligence, the Connecting Leader must also be committed to investing in recruiting and developing a team of reputation intelligence analysts to determine the optimal configuration of the platform and manipulate the data to carry out scenario analysis to find correlations and causality. This requires a fundamental change in mindset, with senior managers—and everyone down the line—internalising a data-driven approach to be equipped with intelligence that leads to confident actions.

SIMPLE AND ACTIONABLE INTELLIGENCE

With robust, evidence-based, real-time intelligence in place, created with data regarding the company and its competitors in all markets and with all stakeholders, companies can further enhance their results by understanding how decisions and actions have created value for the business. This can be achieved through the correlation with third-party data, including business KPIs. This enhancement allows the business to understand how changes in stakeholder perception are genuinely affecting reputation and the value that the company creates.

alva, the business that I founded in 2009, has developed Connecting Intelligence Systems for a number of years in collaboration with its clients. An interesting example is the case of a global mining company, whereby analysing data from a number of regions in multiple languages, the mining company receives alerts on emerging reputational risks for its relationships with local communities at a number of its operational sites. Using a combination of SMS perception, stakeholder engagement and community and media metrics across the group, the client obtains a good understanding of its social licence to operate at an asset-by-asset level.

In a global pharmaceutical company, alva has audited the various primary research outputs for different stakeholders to understand the key drivers of its reputation with these audiences. This knowledge has been used to create a research framework for each stakeholder (issues, expectations, risks and opportunities), which has been embedded into the company's daily monitoring and monthly analysis programmes. Issues known to be impactful for different groups are surfaced quickly to enable the Corporate Affairs team to respond when appropriate.

Having led the Johnson & Johnson Global Reputation Intelligence System, Michael Sneed shares his view: "Our challenges have been two-fold. First, Johnson & Johnson is a large, complex and notoriously decentralized company, so adopting a global approach to anything in a company this diverse is inherently challenging. Second, we needed to ensure that our approach was not overly US-centric. Our stakeholders, and the issues that shape our reputation, exist around the world, so we needed to develop a system that honoured the magnitude of our operations. The good news is, our system has already yielded insights about global issues that were impacting our reputation that had been previously off our radar. Bringing those to light and leveraging them has already resulted in benefits to our enterprise."

Above all, the most important requirements when designing and implementing a CIS are to have clarity on the purpose of the system, consult with different functions to contribute to the design of the system and maintain a very high degree of analysis rigour. Successful reputation intelligence systems have to be simple enough to understand and compelling enough to spur action.

The Connecting Leader Journey

CHAPTER NINE

NOT SO FAST, NOT SO EASY

SO FAR, WE HAVE DEVELOPED AN UNDERSTANDING OF THE New Normal and have examined the increasingly complex role of the Connecting Leader. But how ready are companies to adopt and fully integrate the Connecting Leader role? Is the Corporate Affairs/Communications function the go-to function to take on the increasing demands of operating in today's New Normal? How big is the gap between the current role of the Corporate Affairs/Communications function and the future of the Connecting Leader role?

To find out, we have analysed four regularly published studies: the Measurement Survey from NASDAQ, FTSE 100 Group Director of Corporate Communications/Affairs Survey from Watson Helsby, Rising CCO VI from Spencer Stuart and OCR Senior Corporate Affairs Summit report by Harris. These four publications offer a variety of perspectives on the current state of the Corporate Affairs/Communications function in the United Kingdom, United States and Europe. Where possible, we also provide a global perspective.

To assess the current readiness, the analysis focuses on seven key questions:

1. Is the Director in the post part of the senior executive team?
2. What is the current role remit and its contribution to strategy development?
3. How large is the communication team?
4. Who are the typical business partners or functions?
5. How complete is the integration between marketing and communications functions?
6. How frequently do leaders use analysis and intelligence?
7. What items are on the function's wish list?

The directors surveyed by these four studies represent diverse industries including pharmaceuticals, natural resources, retail, consumer, financial services, energy, utilities, leisure, telecommunications, media, technology and manufacturing. For simplicity, we will refer to the many roles represented under the Communications and Corporate Affairs function as "CAC" functions. These roles include Chief Communications Officer, Senior VP of Corporate Affairs and Sustainability, VP of Corporate Relations, VP of Investor Relations and Communications and VP of External Affairs.

In the final part of the chapter, we will take an outside-in view and review how companies are responding to the current trends in society and how the CAC function prepares the rest of the organisation to take a stand on societal issues.

ACCESS TO THE SENIOR EXECUTIVE TEAM

As we have seen in the earlier chapters, it is critical for the Connecting Leader to have a seat on the senior executive team and work very closely with the CEO as the "Society Proxy." How close are most companies to meeting that goal?

Numbers from the United Kingdom indicate that there is greater access there than in many other markets, as 76 percent of CACs within the FTSE 100 report directly to their CEO and there is broader support for stakeholder-related strategies. This percentage has consistently risen from 2014, when it stood at 75 percent. A closer look at the numbers reveals some nuance. It's clear that the direct communication between a CAC Director and the CEO has increased, but only 51 percent of CACs are formal members of the C-suite, indicating that influence may be limited. On the other hand, that number is up from 43 percent in 2014 and 47 percent in 2015, so we see an upward trend. The number also depends on the size of the company. In the largest companies, the FTSE 20, 60 percent of CACs have a seat on the senior executive team.[142]

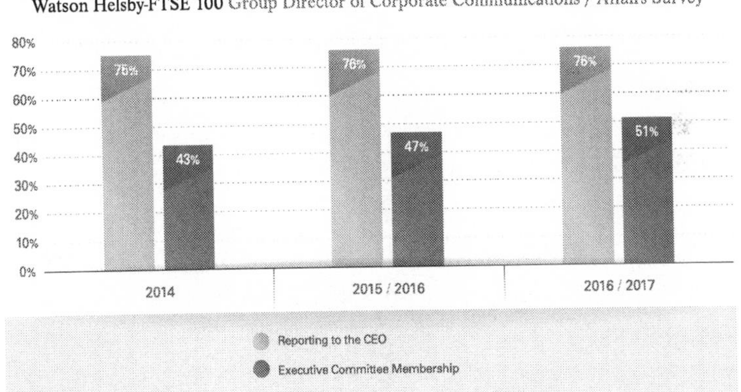

Companies in the United States report senior executive access that looks slightly different from the picture in the UK. In the US,

142 "Watson Helsby. "FTSE 100 Group Director of Corporate Communications/Affairs Survey 2016/17," *The Watson Helsby Report. 2016.* http://www.watsonhelsby.co.uk/insights-and-publications/ftse-100-group-director-of-corporate-communicationsaffairs-survey-201617-results

42 percent of the CAC Directors formally report directly to the CEO and have board access. However, 97 percent of the CACs in the US report working closely with the office of the CEO, even if they aren't directly reporting to them. They may act as advisers, but they don't have the same level of influence as those who report directly. They may have the ear of the CEO, but not the ear of the business as a whole. We found the gap is closing, though; 82 percent of CACs in the US say they expect to work more closely with the office of the CEO over the next few years. This might signal an opportunity for US companies to obtain the same support as their UK counterparts.

In Europe, 48 percent of CACs report directly to the CEO, below the FTSE 100 but above the US market. Ninety-one percent of European CACs report working closely with the office of the CEO and the remaining 9 percent report they "don't work closely with the office of the CEO but would benefit from doing so." Seventy percent of CACs expect to work more closely with the office of the CEO over the next few years.

When we look at the numbers globally, we see that only 43 percent of CACs report directly to the CEO, down from 54 percent in 2014. What's encouraging is that 95 percent of these CACs do work closely with the office of the CEO and the remaining 5 percent report that they "don't work closely with the office of the CEO but would benefit from doing so." Seventy-eight percent expect to work even closer with the CEO and for the relationship to grow over the next few years.[143]

143 Watson Helsby. "FTSE 100 Group Director of Corporate Communications/Affairs Survey 2016/17," *The Watson Helsby Report*. 2016. http://www.watsonhelsby.co.uk/insights-and-publications/ftse-100-group-director-of-corporate-communicationsaffairs-survey-201617-results.

Most Senior Communications Professionals report to...	Region		
	Global CCO's	North America	EMEA
CEO	43%	42%	48%
President	21%	6%	39%
Chief Marketing Officer	6%	6%	6%
Chief Legal Officer	6%	11%	–
Chief Financial Officer	6%	11%	–
Chief Communications Officer / Head of Corporate Affairs / Head of Public Relations	5%	4%	4%
Chief Operating Officer	5%	6%	4%
Chief Marketing & Communications Officer	2%	1%	2%
Chief Human Resources Officer	2%	3%	2%
Business Unit Head	2%	–	4%
Other	14%	15%	11%

Nasdaq CCO Measurement Survey 2017[144]

Overall, CACs are visible to the CEO most of the time. Firms that participated in the most recent Harris Poll, published at the OCR Senior Corporate Affairs Summit, reported that 84 percent of CACs disagree with the statement that "the CEO only pays attention to my team during a crisis." This survey also revealed that 91 percent disagree with the statement "the board often contradicts our policies and suggested courses of action," showing increased trust between the two functions and promising a future with increasing collaboration within the business. Indeed, when asked how their company typically considers whether to

144 Market Insite. "Survey: 101 CCO's on PR Measurement." *Nasdaq*. March 29 2017. http://business.nasdaq.com/marketinsite/2017/Survey-101-CCOs-on-PR-Measurement.html

take a stance or to remain silent, 61 percent of CACs responded that they deliberate within the senior executive team or with the board before announcing a position.[145]

Is it safe to say that the CAC function has the necessary access to the senior executive team? Not yet. However, the increasingly close relationship between the CEO and the CAC function presents an opportunity to lead the conversation within the business, starting from the Executive Committee, on the impact that the company's reputation has on corporate value. When the C-suite recognises how fundamental it is to have a Connecting Leader in the Executive, the influence of the CAC function in the overall business is likely to increase to new highs.

ROLE REMIT

When describing the Connecting Leader role, we identified five specific responsibilities: having the outside-in view and serving as an internal connector, an external connector, a communicator and a reputation risk manager. What do the surveys show and how big is the gap between the current role and the Connecting Leader role?

In the UK, remit can vary considerably for companies in the FTSE 100, which is determined by the sector in which the company operates as well as by the number and diversity of the stakeholders that the company has to engage with. In 2015, 70 percent of CAC Directors had a PR Communications background; in 2017, the numbers show that 59 percent had a PR Communications background. Companies in the UK now hire CACs with a different emphasis. Corporate branding (assigning a purpose and values to a corporation) has become an increasingly prom-

145 The Harris Poll. "The Harris Poll Releases Annual Reputation Rankings for the 100 Most Visible Companies in the US." *Harris Insights and Analytics*. 2016. https://theharrispoll.com/the-harris-pollr-today-released-its-17th-annual-reputation-quotientr-rqr-summary-report-revealing-corporate-reputation-ratings-for-the-100-most-visible-companies-in-the-u-s-as-perceived-by/.

inent component of the role—almost all FTSE 100 CACs are responsible for the corporate brand. Public affairs is more often recognised as an important part of the CAC function, too; companies that tend to operate heavily in regulated industries give significant responsibility for public affairs to the CAC function.

The responsibilities of US CACs vary as well, both within the role and compared to the United Kingdom. US companies emphasise three top responsibilities: media relations (97 percent), crisis management or reputation management (96 percent) and employee communication (90 percent). If we examine the top responsibilities closely, we'll see that they represent a wide variety of tasks, including government relations, data analytics and investor relations. As many as 51 percent of US CACs are also responsible for marketing, branding and advertising. The role is not a simple one and its duties continue to grow. Within the next twelve to eighteen months, US companies expect the CAC role to increase in areas like digital communications (68 percent), reputation management (61 percent) and employee advocacy (70 percent).

In Europe, we also observe highly diverse CAC Director responsibilities. The top three primary responsibilities in the region are media relations (97 percent), crisis management (90 percent) and social media or digital communications (77 percent). Only 70 percent of European CACs report being responsible for employee communications, compared to 90 percent in the US. Also in Europe, 46 percent of CACs have the primary responsibility for marketing, branding, or advertising. The top three responsibilities expected to increase in Europe over the next twelve to eighteen months are digital communications (78 percent), reputation management (67 percent) and corporate identity (52 percent). The bottom three responsibilities for this region include government relations or public affairs (32 percent), data analytics (32 percent) and marketing research and measurement

(12 percent)—the same bottom three as the US. Unlike the US, Europe is not as focused on employee communications.

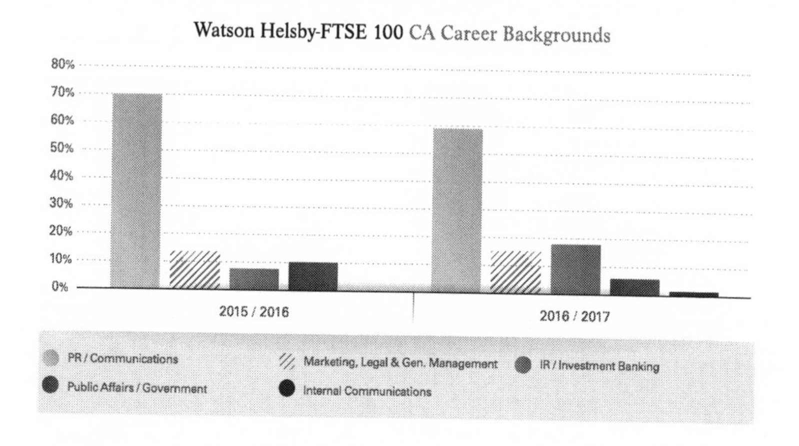

These numbers paint a picture of the evolving role of the CAC and its growing complexity. Among the companies worldwide that responded to the Harris Poll in 2017, 89 percent of CAC Directors agree that their role is more complicated than it was two years ago and 69 percent agree the CAC Director role is often misunderstood.

It's no wonder the CAC role isn't fully understood; the list of responsibilities covers a wide range of areas:

Primary Responsibility	Region		
	Global CCO's	North America	EMEA
Media relations	97%	97%	97%
Crisis management or Reputation management	93%	96%	90%
Employee communications	78%	90%	70%
Social media or digital communications	74%	75%	77%
Corporate Social Responsibility / Corporate Responsibility	57%	61%	56%
Foundation or charitable giving	45%	52%	46%
Marketing, branding or advertising	41%	42%	48%
Government relations or public affairs	38%	32%	46%
Marketing research and measurement	16%	12%	21%
Data analytics	14%	12%	16%
Investor relations	10%	14%	7%
Customer experience	7%	4%	11%

Worldwide, this list of responsibilities is only expected to grow in complexity and importance. Over the next eighteen months, the responsibilities expected to increase include digital communications (72 percent), reputation management (65 percent) and employee advocacy (59 percent). When we look at the KPIs by which the CAC function is measured, the Harris report shows that 90 percent are being measured by outtakes metrics, such as search engine traffic, message pull through, brand awareness, social media shares and audience reach.

Such a complex role can be challenging to measure, report on and analyse. Out of the respondents, 41 percent of the CACs reported their key performance indicators (KPIs) as being too complex to track and 59 percent believe the impact of social media on communications gets harder to measure with each passing year. When asked the three most important KPIs to track, CACs identified customer lead conversion (16 percent), brand awareness (15 percent) and advertising value equivalency (10 percent).

The above numbers indicate a significant gap between the current role, which tends to focus on tactical and reactive activities and the role of an effective Connecting Leader, which takes a big-picture view and provides input regarding the overall strategy of the business, as well as focusing on the outcomes resulting from its decisions and actions. Companies still behave somewhat defensively, when they need to be preparing for the future. Indeed, 49 percent of global respondents said just that, agreeing that they do propose proactive communications strategies but actually spend *most* of their time reacting to the market.

Tactical activities are still important and are necessary responsibilities of the role. However, with access to quality reputation intelligence, the role has the opportunity to provide fundamental strategic insight to the senior executive team and elevate the discussion of key strategic issues.

TEAM SIZE

We've seen that the CAC Director is responsible for a wide range of areas and a team with broad disciplines is necessary. The numbers show that size varies considerably by sector, global footprint and market cap, as well as in-market regulatory and policy-related challenges.

What determines the size and structure of the team? There seem to be four key determinants:

- Global footprint and number of employees

- Complexity and scale of stakeholder relationships
- Breadth of responsibility
- Regulatory and political complexity

In the UK, the FTSE 100 reports that the average size of an FTSE 20 team is 280, whereas the average size of an FTSE 51–100 is only twenty-eight. More specifically, the companies with the largest team headcount are either in the pharmaceutical industry, natural resources, or telecommunications.[146]

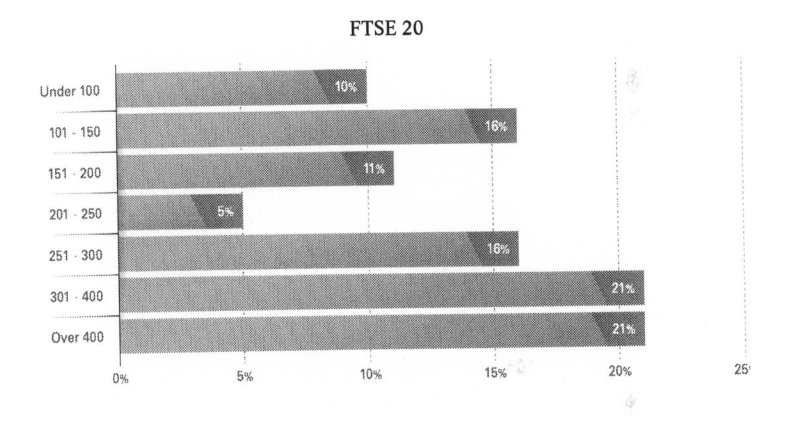

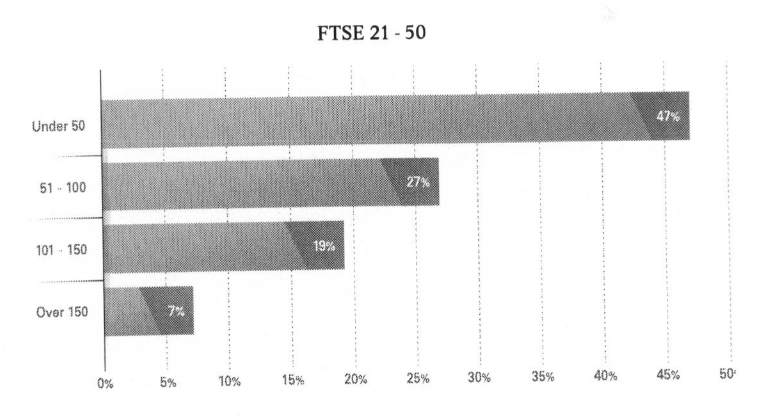

146 Watson Helsby. "FTSE 100 Group Director of Corporate Communications/Affairs Survey 2016/17," *The Watson Helsby Report*. 2016. http://www.watsonhelsby.co.uk/insights-and-publications/ftse-100-group-director-of-corporate-communicationsaffairs-survey-201617-results.

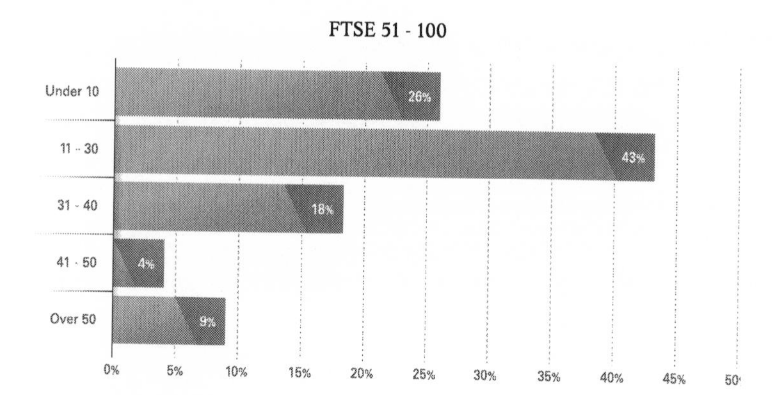

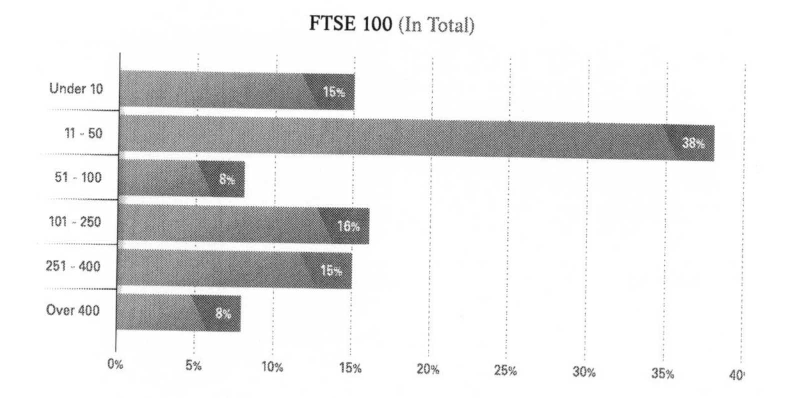

When asked to list the eleven positions a CAC Director will be hiring to fill in the next eighteen months, the surveys show a wide range of roles:[147]

147 M.Giuda and T.McNary. "The Rising CCO VI: Roles and Perspectives of Chief Communications Officers." *Weber Shandwick and Spencer Stuart.* October 5 2016. https://www.webershandwick.com/news/the-rising-cco-vi/

Positions CCO expects department will be hiring within 12-18 months	% Total Responses
Digital manager / Digital communications / Digital marketer	11%
Social media specialist	8%
PR specialist / Media relations manager	7%
Communications head / Manager / Strategist	7%
Employee engagement / Internal communications head / Manager / Specialist	6%
Content creator / Editor / Developer / Strategist	5%
Government relations / Affairs manager, public affairs manager	5%
Data analyst	5%
CSR / Sustainability	4%
Graphic designer	3%
Regional communications	2%

The numbers show that the CAC function is too often thought of as tactical (needing lots of tactical executers), rather than strategic (needing a Connecting Leader). Of particular note is the low level of interest in hiring Data Analysts, which indicates a lack of consideration given to how intelligence informs the rest of the business. Most of the roles put the emphasis on the communications or "narrative owner" discipline, but as we have seen, without the other four disciplines (the outside-in view, internal connector, external connector and reputation risk manager), it is virtually impossible for the CAC function to maximise the opportunity to become a key strategic contributor.

In hiring today, we see recruitment focused on output-based

roles like digital managers, social media specialists, PR specialists and communications managers. It seems to be all about outputs and outtakes with little focus on the strategic component.

BUSINESS PARTNERS

The internal connector (in the Connecting Leader) works in partnership with multiple functions to address issues that affect the whole business. These bridges between functions are being built. In Europe, CACs currently report ten departments as those they work with most closely. The top three departments (excepting the CEO) are digital and social media (95 percent), marketing (88 percent) and human resources (75 percent). The bottom three are research and development (54 percent), customer experience (52 percent) and IT and technology (51 percent). The emphasis is expected to shift in the coming years, with CACs expecting to work more closely with digital and social media (90 percent), customer experience (83 percent) and marketing (77 percent); and less closely with legal (47 percent), investor relations (46 percent) and finance (44 percent).[148]

In the US, the picture looks similar, though US companies express a greater interest in working with marketing and human resources in the future and show less of an interest in working with customer experience than Europe. Currently, fewer US CACs than European CACs work with and intend to work with research and development.[149]

Globally, CACs report forming close partnerships within several key departments.

---

148 M.Giuda and T.McNary. "The Rising CCO VI: Roles and Perspectives of Chief Communications Officers." *Weber Shandwick and Spencer Stuart.* October 5 2016. https://www.webershandwick.com/news/the-rising-cco-vi/

149 M.Giuda and T.McNary. "The Rising CCO VI: Roles and Perspectives of Chief Communications Officers." *Weber Shandwick and Spencer Stuart.* October 5 2016. https://www.webershandwick.com/news/the-rising-cco-vi/

Communications Department currently works closely with now	Department works closely with now			Don't work closely with but would benefit from doing so		
	Global CCO's	North America	EMEA	Global CCO's	North America	EMEA
Office of the CEO	95%	97%	91%	5%	3%	9%
Digital / Social media	92%	94%	95%	6%	3%	5%
Marketing	86%	84%	88%	9%	11%	9%
Human resources	83%	93%	75%	14%	4%	23%
Legal	83%	96%	71%	10%	3%	15%
Government affairs / Public affairs	81%	88%	74%	11%	6%	17%
Investor relations	72%	91%	44%	16%	4%	32%
Finance	70%	82%	55%	16%	5%	26%
IT / Technology	56%	64%	51%	26%	21%	30%
Customer Experience	49%	46%	52%	36%	35%	37%
Research & Development	40%	33%	54%	35%	27%	38%

CACs say they expect their relationships to grow over the next few years with departments as listed above.

Department CCO expects to work more closely with over the next few years	Region		
	Global CCO's	North America	EMEA
Digital / Social media	91%	91%	90%
Marketing	80%	82%	77%
Human resources	79%	81%	77%
Office of the CEO	78%	82%	70%
Government affairs / Public affairs	78%	81%	71%
Customer Experience	76%	70%	83%
IT / Technology	69%	72%	65%
Investor relations	66%	76%	46%
Legal	62%	70%	47%
Research & Development	53%	43%	62%
Finance	53%	58%	44%

When questioned in the most recent Harris Poll about how companies have changed their strategies toward understanding stakeholders, 77 percent reported increasing engagement with employees. Additionally, when questioned about how a company has communicated its stance on certain issues, the number one response (87 percent) was that it communicated to employees directly, showing growing support for communication and integration of values within the business.[150] These numbers send a promising message: CACs are building relationships across the company.

150 The Harris Poll. "The Harris Poll Releases Annual Reputation Rankings for the 100 Most Visible Companies in the US." *Harris Insights and Analytics*. 2016. https://theharrispoll.com/the-harris-pollr-today-released-its-17th-annual-reputation-quotientr-rqr-summary-report-revealing-corporate-reputation-ratings-for-the-100-most-visible-companies-in-the-u-s-as-perceived-by/.

MARKETING AND COMMUNICATION INTEGRATION

Marketing and Communications are no longer siloed as they were ten years ago, when the CAC function was responsible mainly for corporate communication activities. With the emergence of digital channels and content democratisation, both functions have significantly different roles in the business but depend on one another on multiple levels. According to the NASDAQ CCO Measurement Survey, "These two functions are broadening their roles to encompass marketing, PR and social media communications activity and these responsibilities will continue to evolve in a world that is digital-dependent and media-fragmented."[151] Recent trends show the gap between the two is shrinking, with closer collaboration between the CAC function and marketing sometimes leading to complete integration of the two teams. The trend makes perfect sense. One function manages the engagement with consumers or customers and the other manages engagement across all stakeholders.

Within the US, 51 percent of CACs are responsible for marketing, branding and advertising, while 84 percent work closely with the marketing department and 11 percent do not but believe they would benefit from doing so. A full 51 percent report that branding and corporate identity functions will increase focus in the next year, but only 8 percent say marketing research and measurement is expected to be their responsibility going into the next year. Collaboration is strong overall, with 79 percent agreeing that "at my firm, the functions of marketing and communications/public relations are more collaborative than ever." Nearly as many, 49 percent, agree that "at my firm, I expect that marketing and communications/public relations will be fully integrated in the next few years."[152]

---

151 Market Insite. "Survey: 101 CCO's on PR Measurement." *Nasdaq.* March 29 2017. http://business.nasdaq.com/marketinsite/2017/Survey-101-CCOs-on-PR-Measurement.html

152 M.Giuda and T.McNary. "The Rising CCO VI: Roles and Perspectives of Chief Communications Officers." *Weber Shandwick and Spencer Stuart.* October 5 2016. https://www.webershandwick.com/news/the-rising-cco-vi/

In Europe, the research shows that 46 percent of CACs are responsible for marketing, branding and advertising. As many as 88 percent work closely with the marketing department now, while 9 percent report they don't work closely with marketing now but feel that doing so would benefit them. Fifty-two percent report that they expect their focus to increase on branding and corporate identity, but only 12 percent expect to increase their responsibility in market research and measurement. It is rather interesting to see that 63 percent in Europe agree with the statement "at my firm, I expect that marketing and communications/public relations will be fully integrated in the next few years."

The numbers indicate that marketing and communications in US and Europe are similarly collaborative.[153] Globally, there is over 50 percent consensus that the two departments are becoming integrated. Marketing has always been important because of its focus on customer acquisition. As we enter a phase of more socially conscious business, however, people are beginning to realise that though focusing on customer acquisition is fundamental, managing stakeholder relations is equally important. Socially conscious businesses should strive to achieve a healthy balance of both.

ANALYTICS AND INTELLIGENCE

In Chapter Eight, we examined how simple and actionable intelligence is the key to engaging the rest of the organisation to drive change and support opportunities that emerge from stakeholder engagement. When we look at what's happening in business right now, however, we see that most companies are still far from meeting that goal. In fact, the research shows that most compa-

---

153 M.Giuda and T.McNary. "The Rising CCO VI: Roles and Perspectives of Chief Communications Officers." *Weber Shandwick and Spencer Stuart.* October 5 2016. https://www.webershandwick.com/news/the-rising-cco-vi/

nies still conceive of analytics and intelligence in terms of outputs and outtakes, while few of them use analytics and intelligence for strategic purposes. This is a missed opportunity in the UK, the US and Europe.

In the UK, a small number of CACs highlighted the need for better data and data analysis, not just for measurement but to provide better insight to senior leaders and to underpin their recommendations with greater rigour.[154] In the US, 12 percent of CACs are responsible for data analytics and only 25 percent expect data analytics to become an increased function within the department in the next year. In the past year, US CACs have used data analytics to refine marketing messages and company values (85 percent), to evaluate company or brand reputation (82 percent) and to identify online and offline company supporters or critics (73 percent). As many as 71 percent of US CACs currently believe data analytics have been extremely helpful in giving the company better and additional insights and 82 percent expect this helpfulness to increase in the coming three years.

The numbers appear to be improving, but it is quite alarming to see that 61 percent of CACs in the US admit to relying on intuition or gut feeling to make decisions compared to the 38 percent who rely on data analytics.[155]

In Europe, the situation is similar. Thirty-two percent of CACs believe the use of data analytics will increase within the next three years. The department has actively used data analytics within the past year in three ways: to identify online and offline company supporters or critics (84 percent), to evaluate company or brand reputation (82 percent) and to refine marketing messages

---

154 Watson Helsby. "FTSE 100 Group Director of Corporate Communications/Affairs Survey 2016/17," *The Watson Helsby Report. 2016.* http://www.watsonhelsby.co.uk/insights-and-publications/ftse-100-group-director-of-corporate-communicationsaffairs-survey-201617-results.

155 M.Giuda and T.McNary. "The Rising CCO VI: Roles and Perspectives of Chief Communications Officers." *Weber Shandwick and Spencer Stuart.* October 5 2016. https://www.webershandwick.com/news/the-rising-cco-vi/

and company stories (77 percent). European CACs report their top five efforts as: evaluating company or brand reputation (95 percent), refining marketing messages and company stories (95 percent), identifying online and offline company supporters or critics (92 percent), identifying online critics and advocates (91 percent) and improving the customer experience (91 percent).

An encouraging 80 percent of CACs in Europe consider data analytics to be extremely helpful in giving the business better insights and 92 percent believe that data analytics will be essential in giving better insights three years from now. Both US and European CACs expect the helpfulness of data analytics to grow. Interestingly, however, only 44 percent in Europe use data analytics to make decisions. The remaining 56 percent use intuition.[156]

The read from the global perspective is rather different. Only 14 percent of CACs are responsible for data analytics and only 27 percent believe the function will increase its focus on data within the next year. In 2018, only 5 percent of global CACs expect to hire a data analyst for the department.

CACs reported using data analytics in ten categories over the past year.[157]

---

156 M.Giuda and T.McNary. "The Rising CCO VI: Roles and Perspectives of Chief Communications Officers." *Weber Shandwick and Spencer Stuart.* October 5 2016. https://www.webershandwick.com/news/the-rising-cco-vi/

157 Market Insite. "Survey: 101 CCO's on PR Measurement." *Nasdaq.* March 29 2017. http://business.nasdaq.com/marketinsite/2017/Survey-101-CCOs-on-PR-Measurement.html

Activity department has used data analytics for in the past 12 months	Region		
	Global CCO's	North America	EMEA
Evaluate company or brand reputation	81%	82%	82%
Refine marketing messages and company stories	80%	85%	77%
Identify online and offline company supporters or critics	76%	73%	84%
Provide ROI of marketing or communications programs	70%	72%	69%
Identify online critics and advocates	69%	72%	68%
Improve the customer experience	56%	56%	58%
Manage risk	55%	64%	44%
Profile or segment current users / Customers	49%	51%	56%
Identify new customers or markets	45%	40%	51%
Drive product innovation	40%	38%	43%

From this list, we see the majority already use data analytics for evaluating company reputation. In the future, even more will. In fact, CACs expect an explosion in data analytics use over the next few years. They predict data analytics will be used to:[158]

158 Market Insite. "Survey: 101 CCO's on PR Measurement." *Nasdaq.* March 29 2017. http://business.nasdaq.com/marketinsite/2017/Survey-101-CCOs-on-PR-Measurement.html

Activity CCO expects department to use data analytics for three years from now	Region		
	Global CCO's	North America	EMEA
Evaluate company or brand reputation	96%	97%	95%
Refine marketing messages and company stories	94%	95%	95%
Identify online and offline company supporters or critics	90%	90%	92%
Identify online critics and advocates	89%	88%	91%
Provide ROI of marketing or communications program	86%	90%	84%
Manage risk	82%	79%	84%
Improve the customer experience	76%	68%	91%
Profile or segment current users / Customers	76%	72%	86%
Identify new customers or markets	70%	63%	86%
Drive product innovation	65%	64%	72%

Across the board, the awareness of data analytics and their potential use is growing; however, actual use by the CAC function is lacking.[159] Why is that? Leaders know it's important. The technology is here. The tools are here. Yet, the gap remains. We can speculate that some are more comfortable focusing on tactical activities over leading a business transformation, or that there's just a general lack of support from the C-suite.

159 Market Insite. "Survey: 101 CCO's on PR Measurement." *Nasdaq.* March 29 2017. http://business.nasdaq.com/marketinsite/2017/Survey-101-CCOs-on-PR-Measurement.html

WISH LIST/FUTURE FOCUS

As the CAC role's influence increases, the resources it needs to act effectively will need to evolve as well. Looking ahead, people are beginning to acknowledge the need.

In the UK, for instance, when CACs were asked to list their priorities for the year, they cited nine areas:

1. The prominence of the corporate brand due to the importance that companies are assigning to purpose, culture, values and behaviours
2. Political risk and regulatory reform
3. Digital capability and engagement systems to improve their engagement on platforms with all stakeholders
4. Building trust in big consumer brands, where broad societal trust in business has a larger impact
5. Connecting the dots as an integrator within the corporation within all levels of employees in the business
6. Undertaking capability reviews, some using outside consultants and re-evaluating the overall design of the communications function
7. Communicating a new strategy and building a narrative around this
8. Internal communications playing a key role engaging employees
9. Data analysis (although only a small group of companies have highlighted the need for better data to provide senior leaders with better insight)[160]

That's a fairly comprehensive list, but what if CACs had to

160 Watson Helsby. "FTSE 100 Group Director of Corporate Communications/Affairs Survey 2016/17," *The Watson Helsby Report. 2016.* http://www.watsonhelsby.co.uk/insights-and-publications/ftse-100-group-director-of-corporate-communicationsaffairs-survey-201617-results

pick one discipline to focus on? Globally, this is what they would choose.[161]

Area of Focus	% Global CCO's
Reputation	28%
Media relations	7%
Brand / Branding	6%
Building team / Skills	4%
External communications	4%
Corporate culture	3%
Strategy	3%
Customer experience / Engagement	3%
Consistency of messaging	3%

Within this region, 42 percent expect to increase focus on corporate social responsibility and 32 percent expect to increase focus on government relations and public affairs within the next year.

The ultimate definition of the CAC role is clearly still evolving. In the most recent Harris Poll, 69 percent agreed that the CAC role is often misunderstood and 69 percent said that the CAC's

161 M.Giuda and T.McNary. "The Rising CCO VI: Roles and Perspectives of Chief Communications Officers." *Weber Shandwick and Spencer Stuart.* October 5 2016. https://www.webershandwick.com/news/the-rising-cco-vi/

role is underappreciated and assumed to be based on an intuitive understanding of what the market, employees and consumers are looking for.[162]

TAKING A STAND

The CAC role will likely evolve quickly in an accelerating world that increasingly expects companies to take cultural and social stands. More and more companies are having their say in these issues. Several leading companies have decided to speak out this way, publicly demonstrating the role they play in society.

In 2016, for instance, Apple did something remarkable: it came out against an anti-LGBT bill under consideration in the North Carolina legislature. This was the latest—and arguably most significant—stand the company had taken in its growing activism campaign for LGBT rights. While the law itself had no direct impact on its business, the brand activism demonstrated by Apple makes one thing clear: companies are starting to recognise that their customers care not only about what they sell but also about what they stand for and therefore, they're taking stances on social, cultural and political issues.

This trend is hardly limited to Cupertino, California, or even to technology companies. Other corporate powerhouses, including Salesforce and Bank of America, were similarly quick to condemn the North Carolina legislation. What's worth noting in each case is how the companies tackled the issue: with personal, passionate responses from each company's CEO, supported by consistent messaging from communications staff across the organisation.

This kind of corporate activism has been decades in the making. In the New Normal, companies are simply more aware of what

162 The Harris Poll. "The Harris Poll Releases Annual Reputation Rankings for the 100 Most Visible Companies in the US." *Harris Insights and Analytics*. 2016. https://theharrispoll.com/the-harris-pollr-today-released-its-17th-annual-reputation-quotientr-rqr-summary-report-revealing-corporate-reputation-ratings-for-the-100-most-visible-companies-in-the-u-s-as-perceived-by/.

their customers think. The same tools give businesses the opportunity to join issue conversations on equal footing with more traditional advocacy voices. And increasingly, these businesses aim to nurture customer relationships that are lifelong, built not just on product features but also on shared cultural values.

In a study commissioned by the Committee Encouraging Corporate Philanthropy (CECP), 61 percent of companies are sticking to their public advocacy strategy, with more than 20 percent advancing their strategy in response to public reaction to the corporate leaders' stance on social issues. While some companies advocate forcefully, others don't and any approach is subject to public challenge.[163] These findings corroborate national media reports on businesses taking public and legal positions on social issues that affect their employees and threaten their ability to compete and do business effectively. Companies are doing this despite the risk of negative attention from some segments of the public and lawmakers, because of the potential impact on their stakeholders.

Companies that are speaking out regardless of public response say they are doing so because the "issues are important to us or relevant to the business." As Rafael Gioielli, CSR General Manager of Instituto Votorantim, put it, "Considering that society is more aware of the social impacts of a company, we are advancing in our strategy, being more transparent and responsive to our impacts."[164]

Another study from Harris showed that 98 percent of global CACs agreed with the statement, "in disruptive markets it's important to constantly explain why your company matters,"

---

163 CECP. "Leading and Following by Example: Companies Taking a Public Stance on Social Issues." *CECP*.June 6 2017.http://cecp.co/leading-and-following-by-example-companies-taking-a-public-stance-on-social-issues/

164 Daryl Brewster, "Leading and Following by Example: Companies Taking a Public Stance on Social Issues," *TriplePundit*, August 24, 2017. https://www.triplepundit.com/special/commit-forum/leading-following-example-companies-taking-public-stance-social-issues/.

showing there is recognition that companies need to put forth their values when engaging with the public. Furthermore, 91 percent agree with the statement that "the bad corporate behaviours of others provides an opportunity to differentiate and lead," showing when it is beneficial to "take a stand."

The top three reasons CACs believe it is a risk to stand up for a cause are: because it will alienate parts of the customer base (78 percent), because employees don't agree with the stance (61 percent), or because it makes a company look like it is just jumping on the cause for publicity (55 percent). However, 78 percent consider it a risk *not* to speak up because it will appear to the public that they are not "walking the talk," and 56 percent believe being silent will be interpreted as an endorsement of a negative opinion. When asked, "What has your company done in the past year to communicate your stance?" the top four responses were:

- Communicated internally with employees (87 percent)
- Spoken with other companies about taking a group or industry stance on an issue (59 percent)
- Released a formal statement from the CEO or another leadership figure (47 percent)
- Posted on social media from a company account (47 percent)

About half of the respondents (46 percent) agree with the statement "it's difficult to navigate what we should be standing up for in society." However, what shows a change in the attitude is that 59 percent are at least a little more than likely to publicly take a stance on a social issue than they were two years ago, demonstrating that even though there is a lack of information and general confusion from most companies on how to navigate social issues and when to take a stand, the initiative to take a stand has grown. Fifty-nine percent report that when they did take a stance on a social issue, "it went well and was the best thing to do in the situation." However, 24 percent report "it would have been better not to say anything."[165]

SO, HOW BIG IS THE GAP?

There are many exceptional Corporate Affairs Directors and many of them are featured in this book. However, the gap between the vast majority of Corporate Affairs Director roles and the Connecting Leader role described in this book is ample.

The Corporate Affair and Communications profession has evolved dramatically in the last ten years and will change even more in the next five—driven by the New Normal. The scope of responsibilities should expand, while the skills required to be a successful Connecting Leader should be adopted by aspiring professionals.

The profession will continue to grow as it becomes more aligned with marketing and more vital to business. Faced with complex societal issues, the Corporate Affairs professionals will become increasingly ethical, which will positively impact society and attract diverse new talent.

Richard Woods thinks this is a great time for the profession. He says, "It's a great time to be in this role if you embrace the opportunity that's in front of you. The digital landscape provides power to stakeholders and influencers and creates opportunities to engage with them directly. It has the added benefit of enabling us to measure the outcome of this engagement in real time and adjust accordingly. All of this plays to the strengths of communication professionals. Public relations has been a good field to be in for a long time but I think it's going to be even better going forward."

165 The Harris Poll. "The Harris Poll Releases Annual Reputation Rankings for the 100 Most Visible Companies in the US." *Harris Insights and Analytics.* 2016. https://theharrispoll.com/the-harris-pollr-today-released-its-17th-annual-reputation-quotientr-rqr-summary-report-revealing-corporate-reputation-ratings-for-the-100-most-visible-companies-in-the-u-s-as-perceived-by/.

CHAPTER TEN

Connecting in the Fourth Industrial Revolution

WE HAVE EXPLORED THE TERRAIN OF THE NEW NORMAL we're all living in today, but what happens next? In an age of continued acceleration, we can expect this landscape to shift even more and quickly. The future New Normal will result from the coming Fourth Industrial Revolution—the marriage of physical and advanced digital technologies such as analytics, artificial intelligence and the internet of things—and will affect most aspects of life today. While previous industrial revolutions took generations to unfold, the world-changing convergence of wireless connectivity, artificial intelligence, advanced automation, nanotechnology, 3-D manufacturing, biotechnology and big data will now drive change at an unprecedented speed.

Nobody is exactly sure what the Fourth Industrial Revolution will bring. Economists are analysing its impact on society, attempting to forecast whether it will bring about more income inequality or create more opportunities. Scientists are pioneering new capabilities made possible by the collaboration of humans and machines in this new environment. Visionaries describe a brave new world, while also warning of the risks associated with some new technologies, and government agencies are figuring out how best to regulate this new world. The complexity is staggering. To make sense of how all these forces will change the social contract between business and society, business will need to rely more and more on a Connecting Leader to bring the Outside-In view.

In the future, governments and business leaders will be at the forefront of influencing how Industry 4.0 impacts the world. But do they fully understand the impact of Industry 4.0? How will it affect their organisations and workforces? What challenges will they face and what opportunities will they discover? We can gain some insight into these questions by looking at a global research report from Deloitte called "The Fourth Industrial Revolution Is Here—Are You Ready?"[166] The Deloitte research drew on survey results from 1,600 global business and public-sector leaders, as well as multiple one-on-one interviews across nineteen countries. Business and government leaders provided insights into how they and their organisations are positioned with respect to the Fourth Industrial Revolution in four key areas: social impact, strategy, talent and technology.

The report revealed that executives are still grappling with many outstanding strategic issues with respect to Industry 4.0. Their mindset is one of hope mixed with uncertainty—they understand the need to think broadly about all stakeholders and the impact technology will have across organisations and society; but, at the same time, they feel constrained by financial and operational demands, as well as change-management challenges. Executives recognise that one of the biggest threats to their organisations over the next five years is the emergence of new

166 Punit Renjen, "Industry 4.0: Are You Ready?" *Deloitte Review*, January 22, 2018. https://www2.deloitte.com/insights/us/en/deloitte-review/issue-22/industry-4-0-technology-manufacturing-revolution.html.

businesses or delivery models. Yet they admitted having a hard time making the investment case to counter the threat because of a lack of internal strategic alignment and short-term focus. These short-term priorities—the pressure to deliver short-term financial results is significant—have stopped executives from coming to terms with the impending changes. In fact, only 14 percent of the executives responding to the Deloitte survey confirmed they felt ready—meaning 86 percent admitted to not being ready.

Perhaps more concerning, there seems to be a disconnect between a pervasive optimism regarding the expected benefits of Industry 4.0 and what it takes to prepare organisations and workforces to realise the potential of this new reality. According to the survey, C-level executives overwhelmingly (87 percent) said that they believe that Industry 4.0 will lead to more social and economic equality and stability and three-quarters say businesses will have much more influence than governments and other entities in shaping this future. Yet less than a quarter believe their own organisations will significantly influence crucial factors such as education, sustainability and social mobility.

The majority of C-suite executives surveyed confirmed that they will continue to rely on strategies that prioritise traditional business operations rather than taking a broader holistic view of how they can create new value for direct and indirect stakeholders across their organisations. Only 15 percent said they are highly prepared for smart and autonomous technologies and just 17 percent said they are ready for the blurring of lines demarcating industries—all important hallmarks of Industry 4.0.

Business and government leaders increasingly understand that a sea change is coming; however, it's unclear if they appreciate how swiftly it will arrive and what must be done to thrive in the new environment.

WORKFORCE IMPACT: A SERIOUS THREAT

One alarming issue that emerges from the Deloitte study is that global executives appear to be the least focused on the effect on employment. Despite the clear impact Industry 4.0 will have on workforces in every industry and geography, many executives do not express urgency when it comes to tackling the challenges of the future of the workforce. Many jobs and the required skills are destined to change dramatically, though it may be too early to know how or to what degree.

A point of concern is that while only a quarter of the executives surveyed expressed high confidence that they have the right workforce composition and skillsets needed for the future, talent and human resources are at the very bottom of their strategic discussions. Perhaps this is because only 22 percent of respondents believe that the uncertain impact of Industry 4.0 on their workforces will have a significant effect on their organisations. Incongruously, the vast majority of executives still believe they are doing all they can to prepare their workforces for Industry 4.0.

This pervasive perception is unfortunate, due to one of the obvious threats from Industry 4.0—the effect that automation will have on job creation. In a widely noted study published in 2013, Carl Benedikt Frey and Michael Osborne examined the probability of computerisation for 702 occupations and found that 47 percent of workers in America held jobs that are at high risk of potential automation.[167] In particular, they warned that most workers in transport and logistics (such as taxi and delivery drivers) and office support (such as receptionists and security guards) "are likely to be substituted by computer capital" and that many workers in sales and services (such as cashiers, counter and rental clerks, telemarketers and accountants) also faced a high risk

167 "A Study Finds Nearly Half of Jobs Are Vulnerable to Automation," *The Economist*, April 24, 2018. https://www.economist.com/graphic-detail/2018/04/24/a-study-finds-nearly-half-of-jobs-are-vulnerable-to-automation.

of computerisation. They concluded that "recent developments in machine learning will put a substantial share of employment, across a wide range of occupations, at risk in the near future." Subsequent studies put the equivalent figure at 35 percent of the workforce for Britain (where more people work in creative fields less susceptible to automation) and 49 percent for Japan.

We can see the impact of automation on individual industries already. For example, a 2017 graph plotting oil rigs in the United States compared to the number of workers in the oil industry tells an important story.[168] As the number of oil rigs declined due to falling oil prices, so did the number of workers the oil industry employed. But when the number of oil rigs began to rebound, the number of workers employed did not. Drilling, once a dangerous and laborious task, is now automated and requires fewer workers on the ground. New technologies have led to the loss of as many as 440,000 jobs in the global downturn; as many as 220,000 of those jobs may never come back.

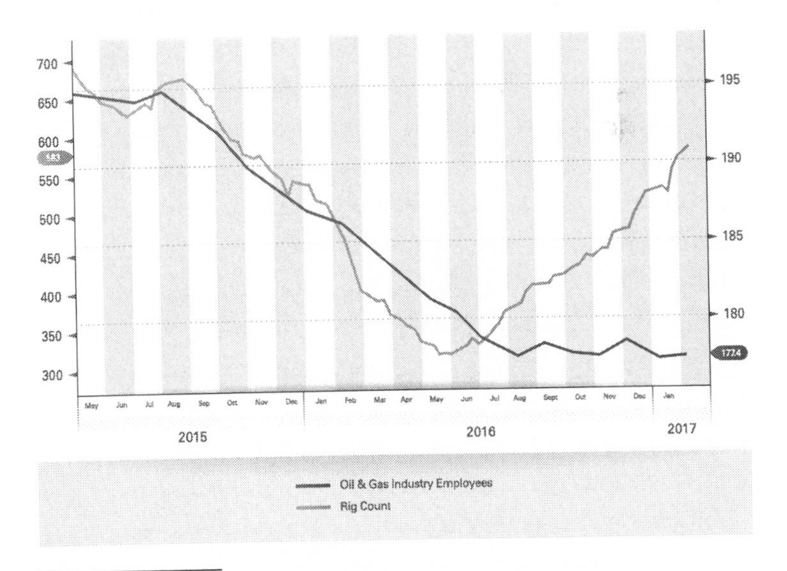

168 Scott Santens."A New Chart Conclusively Proves That Automation Is a Serious Threat," *Futurism*, November 5, 2017. https://futurism.com/new-chart-proves-automation-serious-threat/.

Not only was the change dramatic, but it happened quickly. It only took two years to drive the changes in the oil industry. Why so fast? One could argue that the oil industry didn't really need the workers it lost in the first place. The oil industry used to be extremely profitable without focusing on efficiency, but as "fracking" proliferated and prices plummeted, the industry looked for more efficient ways to run its operations, which ultimately meant that automation removed half of the jobs in the industry.

In the summer of 2016, oil prices were no longer under $30 per barrel and had gone back up to around $50 per barrel where they remain. That's half of the $100 per barrel they used to be, but oil rigs returned to drilling, producing at twice the efficiency with half the workers. Companies will actively invest in automation as it drives operational efficiency. However, what will be the effect on society? Can we believe that everyone unemployed by machines will find better jobs elsewhere that pay even more?

In previous waves of automation, workers had the option of moving from routine jobs in one industry to routine jobs in another; but now, the same "big data" techniques that allow companies to improve their marketing and customer-service operations also give them the raw material to train machine-learning systems to perform the jobs of more and more people.

The history of automation in the computer age over the past forty years suggests that while some with highly valued skills find better jobs, most people end up finding new paid work that requires less skill and thus pays less. The job market is steadily polarising.

Decade after decade, medium-skill manufacturing and office jobs have been disappearing and in response, the unemployed have found new employment in new low-skill service jobs or by taking new jobs requiring higher skill. The middle of the labour market is disappearing. That's the reality and it's been happening for decades.

A landmark 2017 study looked at the impact of industrial robots on jobs from 1993 to 2007 and found that every new robot replaced around 5.6 workers and every additional robot per 1,000 workers reduced the percentage of the total population employed by 0.34 percent and reduced wages by 0.5 percent.[169] During that fourteen-year period, the number of industrial robots quadrupled and between 360,000 and 670,000 jobs were erased.

It's expected that the industrial robot workforce will quadruple by 2025 to seven robots per 1,000 workers. Using Acemoglu's and Restropo's findings,[170] that translates to a loss of up to 3.4 million jobs by 2025, alongside depressed wage growth of up to 2.6 percent and a drop in the employment-to-population ratio of up to 1.76 percentage points.

Predictions that automation will make humans redundant have been made before, of course. In the past, technology ended up creating more jobs than it destroyed. David Autor, an economist at the Massachusetts Institute of Technology, explains that automating a particular task so that it can be done more quickly or cheaply increases the demand for human workers to do the other tasks around it that have not been automated.

Many economists argue that the same pattern can be seen in industry after industry, since the introduction of computers. Rather than destroying jobs, automation has redefined them and in ways that reduce costs and boost demand. In a recent analysis of the American workforce between 1982 and 2012, James Bessen found that employment grew significantly faster in occupations that made more use of computers, like graphic design. As auto-

169 Daron Acemoglu and Pascual Restrepo, *Robots and Jobs: Evidence from US Labor Markets* (MIT, Boston University, 2017). http://www.nber.org/papers/w23285.

170 Daron Acemoglu and Pascual Restrepo, *Robots and Jobs: Evidence from US Labor Markets* (MIT, Boston University, 2017). http://www.nber.org/papers/w23285.

mation sped up one aspect of a job, it enabled workers to do the other parts better.[171]

Computers thus reallocate rather than displace jobs, requiring workers to learn new skills. This is true of a wide range of occupations, Bessen found, not just in computer-related fields such as software development but also in administrative work, healthcare and many other areas. Only manufacturing jobs expanded more slowly than the workforce over the period of study, but that had more to do with business cycles and offshoring to China than with technology, he says.

And while it is easy to predict fields in which automation might do away with the need for human labour, it is less obvious where technology might create new jobs. "We can't predict what jobs will be created in the future, but it's always been like that," says Joel Mokyr, an economic historian at Northwestern University. Imagine trying to tell someone a century ago that her great-grandchildren would be video-game designers or cybersecurity specialists, he suggests. "These are jobs that nobody in the past would have predicted."[172]

So who is right? Is it the pessimists (mostly techie types), who say this time is different and machines really will take all the jobs? Or is it the optimists (mostly economists and historians), who insist that in the end technology always creates more jobs than it destroys? The truth probably lies somewhere in between. AI will not cause mass unemployment, but it will speed up the existing trend of computer-related automation, disrupting labour markets just as technological change has done before and requiring workers to learn new skills more quickly than in the past.

Bessen predicts a "difficult transition" rather than a "sharp

---

171 "Automation and Anxiety." *The Economist*. June 25 2016. https://www.economist.com/special-report/2016/06/25/automation-and-anxiety

172 Hank M. Greene, "Hint: About the Future," *Medium*, March 13, 2017. https://medium.com/@hankmgreene/hint-about-the-future-249bf967e800

break with history." But despite the wide range of prognoses, most agree on the prescription: companies and governments will need to make it easier for workers to acquire new skills and switch jobs as needed. If the pessimists are right and the impact of artificial intelligence proves to be more rapid and more dramatic than the optimists expect, preparing the workforce would provide the best defence.

THE CONNECTING LEADER STEPS IN

As we have seen from the research presented, executives do not feel ready to embrace the opportunities that Industry 4.0 will bring, partly due to the lack of understanding of what the changes actually mean. Today, government is extremely concerned about a number of issues, such as housing shortages, city deals, industrial strategy, digital economy, automation, electric vehicles and 5G. Richard Hamilton believes that "while all these things are going on…companies need to have somebody who's connected into that world and can work out what's going on and how it can frame what they're doing in that world, and that's how you create that distinctiveness."

This is where the Connecting Leader should step in today to help companies for tomorrow. As Nobel Laureate Robert Shiller said, "We cannot wait until there are massive dislocations in our society to prepare for the Fourth Industrial Revolution."[173] The Connecting Leader has the chance to play an even more critical role to engage business with society in a new era that will change the relationship in many aspects of their social contract. Businesses that take time to analyse, assess, organise and act will be better placed to respond to what's coming over the next few years. A truly "tuned in" Connecting Leader should help their

173 Rosamond Hutt, "9 Quotes That Sum Up the Fourth Industrial Revolution," *World Economic Forum*, January 23, 2016. https://www.weforum.org/agenda/2016/01/9-quotes-that-sum-up-the-fourth-industrial-revolution/.

businesses understand what these forces mean and how to act to create social value as well as corporate value.

As we have seen throughout the book, the Connecting Leader is best placed to connect the external and internal worlds. With these connections comes the opportunity to become truly engaged with society and for society to engage with you. With that engagement comes the opportunity to look at the Social Contract in a whole new way, based on your identity and your authentic commitment to society.

As Narayana Murthy, the founder of India's second largest IT sourcing firm, Infosys, says, "Unless a corporation has the goodwill of society, unless a corporation lives in full harmony with all of its constituents, it is unlikely that it will be a long-term proposition. This is true whether it is a developed market or a developing market."[174] The Connecting Leader is the perfect steward to achieve and maintain that harmony.

---

174 John Browne with Robin Nuttall and Tommy Stadlen, *Connect: How Companies Succeed by Engaging Radically with Society* (W.H. Allen, 2005).

CONCLUSION

A CALL TO ARMS

WE'VE CHARTED THE SUBSTANTIAL CHANGES THE BUSINESS environment has experienced in the last fifty years, instigated by a profound societal loss of trust in business as a force for good and accelerated by the New Normal of Interconnectivity, Hyper-Transparency and Media Anarchy.

We've understood that businesses and their leaders need to adapt to this environment and how essential it is to maintain a healthy and balanced contract with society. We've further highlighted the need for companies to reflect on their genuine purpose, to consider their role in society and to ensure that their behaviour, actions and communications are authentically aligned with these.

While change is always divisive, the fundamental shifts we've presented in this volume should be welcomed wholeheartedly. These changes represent the beginning of the end of spin, of duplicity, of inauthenticity.

The rebalancing of power back to society—the re-emergence of the Social Contract—is an overwhelmingly positive development. At its heart, it connects business back to its original purpose, Adam Smith's "forceful engine of societal progress."

While they are currently in the minority, we can see the emergence of businesses that recognise the opportunity that this shift has created—companies such as Prudential Financial, BAE Systems, Rio Tinto and Capital One that are actively fostering harmonious relationships with all key stakeholders, with a full understanding of their Social Contract at the core of their business model, not as an add-on or afterthought.

At the centre of the companies that are thriving in the new environment is one common factor—the Connecting Leader.

The Connecting Leader is the game changer, the compass that enables the CEO to navigate the ever-changing currents of stakeholder opinion and expectations, the bridge across the executives at the top of the organisation and the guardian of the company's integrity in all its dealings.

At its core, this book is a call to arms to CEOs and business leaders to embrace the challenges and opportunities inherent in the changes we've described and to seize the initiative in empowering Connecting Leaders.

For aspiring Connecting Leaders in Communications, Corporate Affairs, Marketing, or any other part of the business, we hope this book can present a clear path to self-empowerment and can equip you with the tools needed to catalyse change in both yourself and your organisation.

While the future will always be unknowable, business performance has and always will be dependent on the support of stakeholders. Having the right Connecting Leader in place is the single greatest step a business can take to ensure its success in the increasingly complex world of the New Normal.

Acknowledgments

THIS BOOK COMES OUT OF TWENTY-FIVE YEARS FILLED with experiences, lessons and exchanges with many people who have generously shared with me (consciously or unconsciously) their wisdom, their ambition and their affection. Each and every one of them has inspired me and supported me on that long journey. My first thanks go to Gina Melillo, my assistant and researcher, who with diligence, rigor and a positive outlook has gone far beyond the call of duty to ensure that this book happened.

Many ideas in this book have grown out of discussions I have had in a range of countries over the last ten years with alva colleagues, clients, business opinion leaders, corporate executives, academics and university students. Thank you all—and particular thanks to everybody who agreed to be interviewed for the book and whose insights and knowledge were key to creating the Connecting Leader framework: Lauren Day (Prudential), Ken Darby (Thales), Claire Divver (BAE Systems), Nigel Fairbrass (Eterna Partners), Richard Hamilton (KPMG), Nick Helsby (Watson Helsby), Peter Mitic (University College London), Simone Niven (Rio Tinto), Robin Nuttall (McKinsey & Company), David Oliver (Mondelēz International), Wylie Rogers (Tantalus Group),

Michael Sneed (Johnson & Johnson), Richard Woods (Capital One) and David Woolwine (Allstate Insurance).

I would like to also thank alva for allowing me the time for the Connecting Leader project. Especially I would like to thank my business partners, Alastair Pickering, Richard Fleming and Richard Goldsmith, for joining me in creating the business that alva is today. We had no idea what alva would become and through hard work, strength and humility we have created a business to be proud of.

I am extremely grateful to Andrew Vickerman for being my mentor and a friend over the last ten years and to Bill Haney for his continued wisdom and direction. Thanks also to the support from Charles Lewington, Quentin Boyd, Jeremy Lehman and Oliver Thomas from Grafton Capital, and to Nick Badman, Jane Reoch, Helen Reynolds and Peter Cullum from the Cass Entrepreneurship Fund.

I greatly appreciate the support and love I have had from friends over the years, among them Afroditi Forti, Mike Panteli, Derek Morgan, Sheena Shah, Julian Dench, Andy Taylor, Giles Drury, Nicola Harley, Dominic Sharp, Mark Rigby, Chris Clark, Lauren Day, Sergio Maldonado, Jordi Pique, Rommel Johnson and Antonio Bauza. Thank you for always giving me the encouragement to be better.

I am deeply grateful to my parents, Lucas and Maria Dolores and to my brothers, Manolo, Jose Antonio, Carlos and Javi. Special thanks to my beloved sister, Esther, one of my biggest inspirations.

Last and most, thank you to my partner in life, Madalina, without whose love, kindness and full-time parenting I would have never written this book. And to our daughter, Alma, who like all children deserve to live in a world of freedom, fairness and endless opportunities.

About the Author

For over twenty-five years, Alberto Lopez Valenzuela has worked in business information and analysis, developing decision-intelligence solutions for Fortune 500 companies. He held roles in marketing, strategy and corporate development at numerous global enterprises before founding and serving as Chief Executive at alva, a technology-enabled company that creates decision-ready intelligence for the largest companies in the world. Alberto is a visiting professor at Cass Business School, where he earned his MBA and holds an honours degree from the University of the Arts London. He splits his time between alva's offices in London and New York.